Fornication Under Carnal Knowledge

G. Leon Dunbar

authorHOUSE®

AuthorHouse™
1663 Liberty Drive
Bloomington, IN 47403
www.authorhouse.com
Phone: 1-800-839-8640

First published by AuthorHouse   03/03/2011

ISBN: 978-1-4567-4604-9 (sc)
ISBN: 978-1-4567-4605-6 (e)

Contents

CARNAL - CARNAL - CARNAL - CARNAL - CARNAL - CARNAL

KNOWLEDGE - KNOWLEDGE - KNOWLEDGE - KNOWLEDGE

<u>Foreword</u>

Yes, you have been screwed and long before your conception. The wrong choices were made for you and you continue to make wrong choices now. It is time that you start to change this.

These are my ideas, affirmations, dreams, visions, and opinions. I am detailing how you can begin to change yourself. The process of changing self is a journey I have been on for a long time and one worth continuing. I am asking that you join me.

Introduction

President Roosevelt once said that American presidents are elected at barbershops. Well, as ironic as that may seem to some readers, political leaders representing every niche of society are indeed elected there.

The barbershop is an institutional reservoir of knowledge and information. The reason this is so is that it is the only place where men, women and children, from every level of society, can come and vent, discuss and debate ideas and opinions, freely exchanging information, as well as receiving differing views from those reared within their own neighborhoods as well as from people raised throughout the lands. All for the price of a haircut.

I freely associated with my customers for the many years I barbered. They views and opinions helped to stimulate my and to inform my inquiry into the mysteries of life. Realizing that the majority of the people throughout the world are living under the auspices of freedom has propelled me to share the knowledge I have struggled to acquire.

Fornication under carnal knowledge has been and will continue to be an intellectual, egotistical campaign to control the mind and direction of humanity. This obscure and diabolical campaign has one purpose: to rob humanity of the loving Spirit of the true God.

The word "fuck" is merely an expression of resistance to spiritual invasion. "Fuck" is an alarm that sounds whenever that Christ-space has been impaired. Said space is intended to be the reservoir of self-love while the egotistical campaign is designed to separate humans from love.

Submitting to egotistical energy is to lose self-control. Submitting to the ego, hence forgetting yourself, makes you a puppet to everything that the ego can provide: they are only toys. Yes, you have been screwed.

I believe it would be grossly unfair to write a book indicting social abuse, pain, frustration, and confusion without including my own personal experiences.

I am George Leon Dunbar, a male born into the post-slavery, segregated southern United States, born into a matrix I was unaware existed. Naturally, I knew nothing about the social mold into which I would be formed. As I matured and became aware of my environment, I realized how little my parents knew, yet they were the ones responsible for my social development.

I dedicate this book to my family and to the Hip Hop culture. Your confusion, frustration and destruction are justified. You knew no better. However, after reading this book, you will. Then it will be your responsibility to change.

In order to illuminate the need for humanity to change, I offer you this book, as it will provide you with many impressions, vibrations and researched opinions concerning the origins and multiple manifestations of the ego campaign.

PROLOGUE:

Early Living and Styles

During the evening, when I was just a child living in the deep and dark rural south, my grandparents would sit my siblings and me in a large circle on the floor and would tell us of our history and the stories that had been passed down to them. Some of the stories interested me while others did not yet I always found the process of storytelling exciting. So, I have always been enthusiastically committed to understanding the reasons why the African and the African American are in the social conditions that we are presently. While researching the phenomena periodically throughout my lifetime, whether through literature or orally probing others, the responses to my inquiries are always the same: social prejudice, greed and economic selfishness, which have and which will always prompt unrest and uprisings. You would think that by now (2010) we would understand and appreciate human commonality. We all hurt, pain, bleed, get hungry, and die the same way even though we enter life in the guise of a multitude of shapes, sizes and colors. We only belong to a single race, the human race. To ignore that fact is to be socially retarded, ignorant or downright stupid. However, we should all know by now that the ego can, it has and it will continue to take you there, to the very door of dumbness.

The ego continues to deceive humans into believing that they are better than another is. This repetitive game of greed and selfishness instigates distance between man and woman, parent and child, family members from one another, ethnic groups from each other, and nation from nation. The socio-economic and political game gives some humans a little bit of the nations' (substitute state / county / city / family) wealth, an action that serves to marginalize those who are unfairly deprived.

If you were the lowest on the social economic scale, you got little or nothing. Grandparents told me that these deprived conditions forced them to make do with whatever they could get their hands on. They would kill wild life for their meat, plant their own crops (when they could afford to buy the seeds), build their own homes from trees they cut down or from old lumber when they could find some. They formed subdivisions and very close communities. A few of these subdivisions became towns owned and controlled by Blacks. Many of these towns flourished until the former slave owners wanted the land back.

Sometimes, Master had a legitimate though selfish reason for taking "his" property back, but other times, he took it back just because he could; raping the former slave of his masculinity and, oftentimes, raping the wife and daughters as well. Having no legal rights, the post-Emancipation slave could do nothing but to accept the punishments, be prosecuted or to die.

These actions and reactions had a devastatingly profound and negative effect on the Negro, especially the man. In the face of his family, he was made to feel inadequate, helpless, defeated and worthless. These conditions, over a period, create inferiority complexes, attitudes and mindsets that plague and that haunt the Negro to this day. Nevertheless, somehow, they survived. With a strong community, bound and convicted to God, they survived. However, much damage had been done, especially to the family unit. The position was devastated. He would never feel completely protected or able to protect another. This impairment is evident even today.

Because of their survival, the master had to change and to step-up his game. The ego is capricious and is dedicated to its selfish, controlling mission. The Super Egos began allowing education and jobs to a very limited few, knowing that this would create despair, anger and hatred among the newly freed ex-slaves. Master did not stop there. The Super Egos then empowered the Negro woman over the Negro man in order to create strife within their households.

The Super Egos used complexion as a wedge. If light in complexion or damn near white, you could get a job or receive a promotion. Because of the financial stability either of these two economic positions afforded, these ex-slaves could live better lives. They were thereby allowed a few of the luxuries that Master owned and could better assimilate into American society, oftentimes moving away from their fellow negroes because they felt they were better. In this way was the privileged Negro trapped: he could not go back to help the brother (lesser) Negro for fear of losing his job and social status. The inability of the privileged to help the lesser empowered left a void wherein bloomed the seeds of distrust in Negro relationships that continues until this day.

It has been proven, by many scholars and universities, that deprivation and stress have a direct effect on biological and mental structure of the human. This social disease of inferiority still exists and still affects many young African Americans today. It has also infected many young Caucasians, and the youth of other ethnicities, as well. We live in a world where most people have little self-esteem. With all of modern technology, these people are still not exposed to the things needed in order to help them meet tomorrow's rapidly growing changes. This permeating lack of self-esteem is not good or promising for the future of the world. You could say that the chickens have come home to roost.

Inferiority is a social, infective disease that cannot be controlled or destroyed, unless the Super Egos let the divine spirit of true love enter into the socio-economic political processes. We as human beings must learn to share not some but the entirety God has given us. In addition, if we do not, we will not have to worry about someone or anything fanciful destroying us because, if we do not change, we will destroy ourselves.

The information and the historical accounts my grandparents gave me has been helpful. That information has aided me in understanding the African-American condition as well as me. Hence began my journey back to my spiritual self.

This book is not intended to indoctrinate, to direct or to misdirect. It has been written simply to suggest different thoughts. It is based on my spiritual affirmations, dreams, visions, and lifelong experiences. It is a culmination of my committed attempt to stimulate another point of view. I would also like to call attention to the Hip Hop mindset and culture, with the hope that they get a better understanding of the many reasons "why" that have never been addressed.

I have much disdain for Hip Hop, a musical art form that has flourished for more than 20-years. I cannot appreciate the hostile feeling and the anger that is expressed in its compositions, yet I do understand why so many artists use these expressions.

It is my belief that man, at its origin, was a being that had the capability to transform itself from a spiritual, invisible being into a physical being at will. However, for some reason, man became obsessed and consumed with the physical and thereby lost contact with his connection to the spiritual. My reasons for believing such are spawned by my life-long observations of myself and of other men.

The psychological factor in the human (the brain or the mind) is only a recorder. It merely records what it has experienced. What I have recognized throughout my experiences and the experiences other men have shared with me is that humanity is constantly trying to go back to its spiritual self. Moreover, the more a man tries to return, the more difficult the journey becomes. Why? Man's greatest obstacle along the path of return is his own material mind. He wants his cake and to eat it, too.

In order to return to his spiritual origins, man must relinquish his obsession with his selfish materialistic world and submit to the divine spirit of oneness. This is the only way he can ever again achieve completion. Unfortunately, the Hip Hop culture emerged during a time in our society when we were collectively consumed with materialism, void of true love and of spiritual substance.

I was raised in South Carolina subject to the philosophy to "be the lesser of two evils." My mother always told me this, which was confusing because, in my reasoning, if I made a choice I was still choosing evil. My attempt to adhere to my mother's instructions awakened me to the fact that my parents knew that what they themselves were teaching me was, too, evil, but that they had decided that their evil was lesser, and that was all right. Therefore, as I grew, I learned that evil better and better. Later, when I became good at being evil, as well as my parents had taught me to be, I began doing "evil" to others as well as to myself, things like smoking, drinking, eating unhealthy foods, and ingesting drugs. We lie to bill collectors; we lie to our neighbors about our social-economic condition and status, etc.

I remember when I first started feeling horny. I had to lie to myself, as I'd been lied to by the adults of the town I lived in, trying to convince myself, or to convince them that they were correct in informing me that I was too young to have those feelings of arousal. Therefore, I tried to assure them that I understood and wholly accepted the impending ramifications for ever feeling the need to express those feelings of desire (as if I dared): God would have cursed me. As bad as early adolescence was for me, I knew that my poor sisters had it much worse.

Because the female matures faster than the male, they really went through the hormonal ringer. They had to become REALLY good liars. Moreover, and worse of all, at the onset of their sexual maturation, when their reproductive organs were developing within their bodies, they had to deny and to suppress all outwards signs of said development, lest they be considered "fast", "loose" or "womanish." All of these labels which, once placed there by the society within our small town, would have lasted forever and have caused my parents to punish their daughters. Moreover, I believe that by suppressing all of their feelings concerning this development can cause a young woman to suffer mental disorders, a belief that is supported by modern psychology.

Modern medicine indicates that prolonged repression and suppression of any desire creates stress, anxiety, insomnia, and a number of other unhealthy conditions. Now consider having to suppress and repress what is naturally occurring to human kind from approximately the age of 11 until marriage and then you can begin to understand the difficulties my sisters experienced daily. In addition, the adult men of the town would often tell me things like "get as much as you can" whereas my sisters were constantly hearing that they'd better "keep your legs closed and your panties up until you are married". These are the kinds of lies that create imbalances in our social strata and that perpetuate the continuation of evil within our society, i.e. boys verses girls.

In truth, all animals in captivity, once they reach the state of puberty, respond to their natural biological instincts, except for the human being. It is no wonder anyone within my town survived their own adolescence. What is most interesting about the socialization of the human being back then is that both my grandmother and great-grand mother followed the laws of nature concerning their desire to marry and to mate. In that time, it was normal for women to marry by their early teens. In fact, any woman who remained unmarried by the age of 20 was considered an Old Maid.

It is my belief that these conditions were changed so that the Super-Ego could exert more control over society. It is a fact that if woman has multiply sexual relationships before they get married, it is more difficult for them to submit to the tradition roles they have had to fulfill, those of mother, of dutiful wife and of caregiver. Therefore, the Super-Ego, in order to create confusion and discontent, created liars and sneaks of the women while promoting to the men to get as much as they could, creating liars of them as well.

Hence, the continuation of the ever-repeating game of the lesser of the two evils. This game if not played masterfully, could eventually isolate the woman from her parent's grace if not from their home altogether. Being put out of the home could eventually affect the economic processes of this country as these daughters, and granddaughters sought fulfillment of their basic needs through material conquest. As their husbands had already been taught to function as providers by working outside of the home, they were soon joined by the daughters of repression seeking their fulfillment in material acquisition, both actions now having culminated into a society wherein the child is left home alone to raise him or herself.

Problem is, today's children, with all of their toys, with access to information and the world being much smaller than it seemed to be in my great grandmother's time, still experiences puberty. Children are still denied the right to healthy expression of their natural feelings, in a world filled with churches that still refuse to provide them with any true spiritual guidance, thus continuing to invalidate the child's God-given biological vibration. All is consumed with evil.

This book is dedicated to all of the hypocrites, those physical and spiritual abusers that use the word "Fuck" yet who deny their usage of it as well as the popularity of the word.

Fuck is the most popular word used by English speaking people. Yet it is deemed as being derogatory, disrespectful and otherwise foul. It is never given its respect for its spiritual substance. Fornication is abuse. Rape is abuse. Each of these acts signifies acts of violation of the spirit.

This extremely ambiguous and abstract word, "fuck", can be used in many ways and for a mountain of many things. I will attempt to set the record straight. First, fuck is the foremost expression that is closest to the abuse of our human spiritual presence. Once we humans feel that our spiritual presence has been violated or impaired, we respond with the expression "fuck", or "fuck it" or "fuck you", which only means that someone has violated one's spiritual self:

F – Fornication (rape is when any human
is forced against its will to satisfy the
desire of someone else),

U- under (subject to, by way of false
pretense),

C- carnal (man-made, of the flesh); non
spiritual

K- knowledge (miss-information for the
purpose of control); information to prevent
one from true self-reliance

I have repeatedly asked myself whether I should write this book. The answer that comes to me, from deep within myself, and is supported by outward vibrations is resoundingly "yes". I write this book because there is someone out there who is feeling and thinking about the same things about which I am writing. Why? Why am I confused about myself? Where are the answers? Why can't someone give me answers that are not steeped in selfishness and control-oriented? Why don't I like myself? Why are people so angry, deceptive, and self-destructive? The answer to all of these inquiries is simple: The system.

The system is designed by evil to promote evil, to promote separation of individuals from themselves, from their spiritual content, thus from their Creator. The system, ultimately, is man's desire to become God, a God to support his abusive, selfish control, deceiving the masses that subscribe to said system, using the lesser of the two evils predicament.

The human Super Egos, knowing that they could not get the support from the spiritual loving God of oneness, turned their aspirations into themselves, thus becoming Gods of their own creation. This was the beginning of endless confusion and the beginning of the word "fuck". As a response, "fuck" is an expression of human outrage, used most appropriately when the space that the loving God of Oneness occupied becomes invaded by man's selfish and egotistical system. Upon submission to said system, you yourself become subject to fornication-under-carnal-knowledge.

Read this book while trying to understand what all of this means.

FORNICATION - FORNICATION - FORNICATION - FORNICATION

Father Forgive Them

Mothers and Father have been lied to,
Teaching their children the same lies too,
We cannot blame them, for they had to do what their masters told them to.
Suffering little children trying to find their way, many of them have gone astray,
Some not even knowing where their parents live or stay.
Misdirection their only voice,
The lesser of two evils their only choice.

Father forgive them, for they know not what they do,
They have been lied to,
They have been denied the real you.

Mothers and fathers working day and night,
Trying to satisfy a social appetite,
Leaving their children home, alone,
Children raising themselves, on their own.

Father, forgive them, for they know not what they do.

The rich worship fortune and fame,
The poor work themselves to death, trying to stake their claim.
Love-starved babies die while the world stands by, turning their heads and asking why.

Heavenly Father, let the divine light of love come shining through.
Show them material value is not of you.
Unconditional love for your human brother is the only way to satisfy you.

The Social Play on Words-Fornication

Man	Assuming total responsibility of environment	
Woman	Woe unto man	
God	Guard	
Jesus	Justice	
Lord	Lord	Layer
Eve	Evil	
White	Light	Knowledge
Black	Dark	Without knowledge

Hip Hop as a Social Movement

This section of my book is dedicated to a social movement. For many years, I held much disdain for the Hip-Hop culture. This art form is a musical expression that made me, and many of my age, very uncomfortable and left us in wonder. Most of us did not think or believe that Hip Hop would last for more than a few years. Twenty+ years later, surprisingly, history has proven us wrong.

We asked ourselves many questions about this musical enervation. While the form itself is abstract, the antics displayed by many of its artists and devotees are extremely disrespectful and distasteful to most adults. However, both form and antics are entertaining and musically seductive to our youth.

Most decent-minded adults felt that Hip Hop was merely another platform to devalue and to dismantle all that we, the adults, had fought to gain during the battles for equality within this nation, circa 1955 – 1968. "That music is so angry" was often heard and agreed upon whenever adults discussed the emergent art form. That was 20 years ago. Little could we have forecasted that the most devastating and lingeringly negative impact Hip Hop would have would be on the children, too young to think for themselves, those lacking true parental direction and family support; another result of the cultural saturation of Hip Hop.

These children, many of whom by the age of 12 are wholly consumed by their Hip-Hop-infected egos, are mimicking the attitudes and the antics of an ego-dominated society.

The ego even has a look for each age group. For the young, there is a look and a fashion. There is the same for young adults and there is even one for older adults. Yet, of all looks and fashions promoted by the super ego, the innocent youth are the ones most targeted for corruption via the constant taunt to adopt attitudes and items (toys) designed to grant them false understandings. The youth are the most victimized because they are not mature enough to know themselves, that they are not responsible enough to behave and to dress in accord with their own safety, hence in ways that will stabilize their present lives and, ultimately, the futures. The whole-hearted and energetic application they give to acquiring their selfhood is not supportive of themselves, thus is does not support Creation. The youth are the most used and manipulated.

This ego-driven system sells them anything, regardless of how ridiculous the fashion or the fad is, allowing them to believe that the fashion or fad is them and that they created the look. Then, after it has sucked all the monetary value out of the item or action it previously promoted, usually after much social damage has been done, the Super Egos pass laws and rules against the fad, just as they are currently doing against the plastic fantastic world of Hip Hop.

Plastic fantastic is a man made system of falsehoods and lies. Hip Hop, the movie industry and all forms of entertainment are responsible for this social condition. Many people are committed to this mission and are being paid, very well, to further this condition by creating images, characters and unreal scenarios that, for the most part, can never be achieved or accomplished by most viewers.

People of all ages, young and old, even the elders of society are addicted. They are endlessly committed to creating, within themselves, these images and these false lifestyles. These musicians, movie stars, athletes and entertainment icons are often described with adjectives like the "most beautiful," the "most exciting," the "most talented," etc. Children are bombarded and seduced by these images at very early stages in their lives, never given a chance to get to know their real true selves. This process fuels a multi-billion dollar industry, the selling of hair, cosmetics and all manner of toys to edify a plastic fantastic society.

Man does not actually control anything within his artificial system, which super egos fix and repair daily. Neither man nor ego could ever control anything as beautiful and wonderful as the order called nature. Both man and ego are too selfish. Yet man tries to convince himself that he is not selfish.

Nevertheless, let us imagine if man did control all of nature. Only certain groups of people would have everything while other groups would have nothing. Man would be charging people for air and sunlight. He already charges us for water. And what a mess he has made of it. Just imagine paying to breathe air and to feel the warmth of sunlight.

Water was given to all of creation by the Creator but man has taken control of the water supplies. Some men, the super egos, get rich controlling and selling water while others die of thirst. The super ego would cut off your air and sunlight if you fell behind on those bills. The world would be a bigger disaster. Man's system is artificial and plastic yet it is as real as life itself to an artificially intelligent mind.

Man has become like a child on Christmas Day. He has many toys. Toys he must have to make himself feel like he has created something, in his quest to make himself believe that he is competing with Creation. Man's ego will not allow him to believe that Creation is complete.

Man would like to be in control of creation and life. This is the never-ending mission of his ego, but he will never be. He is too selfish and he has separated himself from the most powerful force in the universe. Love is the energy that holds all things together, never destroys or separates.

This manic ball of energy called man is restless, after having accepted his ego, because he now has no solid foundation. He is anchored in himself and he glorifies himself by investing in more toys.

It has been my lifelong quest to understand why humans with everything, including plenty of toys, are not happy and never seem satisfied. I am certain that most of you reading this book have wondered the same. Well, I will attempt to explain and to help you to understand why they are not happy.

First, in order to achieve any understanding of this social mystery, you must recognize that the natural loving spirit of life has been invaded. This invasion took place time immemorial. What makes this invasion so difficult for humans to understand is that it was not a direct attack on the physical, it was not taught and it was not talked about properly. "Proper" so that all humans can understand what they are dealing with in their struggle to survive.

This invasion was deliberate and very much like the social invasion of today, but it was much more committed and determined: obscure, absolute and immensely devoted to destroying the loving Oneness. This was an invasion of energy. Energy is a negative force that evolves from deliberate resistance to the unified loving Oneness of Creation. That friction is also called evil or ego: the going away from God or etching God out.

This parasitic yet invisible predator is energy that runs parallel to the loving spirit of Oneness. It has no life source of its own. Because it depends on the spirit of love for its life source, it is often mistakenly accepted for the loving spirit of the true Creator.

This energy shares similar characteristics with the loving creative spirit, but is far from being the same. This energy has created its own world, a world of glamour and bling-bling, wherein everyone does what they wish without respect for self or for anyone else. It is a world of self-absorption and self-destruction.

Well, after all that has been said, I must admit that most humans in our society today seem committed to the negative, self-absorbed 'I want more' direction. The super egos of the world just take and take, not because they need to do so in order to promote the betterment of humanity. They take to satisfy their own selfishness, which prompts them to deprive the masses of lesser egos, prodding them into an intense state of need, while removing from the lesser egos their basic life survival resources.

Then, after they have pillaged and raped the resources of the lesser egos, Super Egos flaunt and dangle their ill-gotten spoils in the faces of the extremely deprived, ignorant, ill exposed, needy, and greedy. This process promotes desire that ultimately forces the ones deprived to continue the same diabolical attitude and mission, to achieve, unfortunately, without proper resources.

This diabolical form of exposure becomes a recruiting campaign for the legacy of the negative, artificial, parasitical energy, while the rich get richer and the poor destroy themselves trying to stake their claim. It is a process that is promoted and is carried-out daily by various forms of media: music, movies, television, books and magazines.

The exposure of the rich and famous to those who never had a chance to attain said glamorous lifestyles is diabolical, as are most that are willing to do anything to be a part of this evil process. Many innocent and naïve people have been consumed by this taunting social process without even knowing they are ensnared, hence, continuing the legacy.

All of my life I have watched people ensnared within their obsession to chase the big thrill, myself included. The chase starts with our physical and sexual attributes and extends to our material possessions and to our religious convictions.

The human being has an intense desire to be the most powerful and the most beautiful and, in some cases, the most intellectual. He (the human) not only wants to be the best that he can be for himself, but he is, too often, consumed with appearing to be better than anyone or anything else, not just in his immediate circle, but in the entire universe. He just has to have it all.

The human cares less whether his desire to control is righteous, whether it is for the benefit of the masses, or whether, in acting on his impulse to take a chance within his environment, he runs the risk of losing his life or the lives of others. He must be in control of everything. It is the tremendous energy he exerts, in his efforts to control of everything, which I have labeled "the big thrill."

As he travels this journey of thrills, man continuously desires to become bigger and better. He then becomes obsessed with this quest, so much so that he does not realize that most of the things he is trying to conquer or to take control of: 1) he truly does not need, 2) for the most part, these things are not to his benefit, and 3) he actually destroys them in his attempt to acquire them. He just wants control.

At this point of obsession, the act of sharing is not part of his being. Unfortunately, this game of thrills is played daily within families throughout this country. The thrill of conquering the minds of American children, spouses and other family members is epidemic and, in most cases, the deception and manipulation of those closest to us, for our own selfish benefit, overshadows our collective efforts to be daily living examples of love. This omission only comes back to haunt us because the human mind is constantly changing and being influenced at home as well as away from parental / familial guidance.

After the adult introduces deception and manipulation to the family, then, these lesser egos adopt these energies and exert control within their own microenvironments. Haven't we all seen bullying from the time we first entered elementary school?

It is usually only after the alleged adults, the dispensers of the negative energies into the homes, receive a taste of the big thrill (deception and manipulation in order to control) from those close to them, be it spouse or child, when these adults are made to understand that they are not actually in control of anything.

At this point, the adult realizes that they no longer have control and they need and seek help but are unable to find anything, short of more big thrills, to sustain or pacify these self-created situations.

Situationally speaking, the artificial man has divested himself of true love and of spiritual substance. His truth is founded in science and his material world: greed, control, selfishness, and fear. Fear because he has no one to rely on but himself and his material world. Therefore, he conquers and controls everything that he deems a threat to self and, if he cannot control it, he will destroy it. And I mean everything.

To appease himself, man has created a God, in his own image, to please him and to support his material world, complete with all of his selfish, controlling and greedy characteristics. This God gives him what he wants and he will always want more! Why? Because man is a worshipper of his own flesh and of materialism, neither of which lasts very long.

So, man is always looking and searching for something or anything to prolong his distraction with his flesh, even reducing the image of man to buffoonery: wearing over-sized pants, sideways hats, brogan shoes at the height of Summer sans socks, usually topped with leather and wool sweaters, though clearly out of season.

The Hip Hop icons, walking and talking though clearly not lovingly thinking billboards promoting the images of man's buffoonery, were innocent and were obviously ignorant of their oppressed and deprived pasts, and the ugly and often violent struggles that their predecessors endured in order to gain human respect.

In fact, super egos offered them the illusion that they could be on top without ever leaving the bottom, without the foundation required to realize that a solid cultural base, one filled with love and respect for each other, is required before a person can truly ascend to the top. What is not required is money, bling-bling, nor the annihilation of one's brethren. These icons promote the abuse of and disrespect toward their own women and children, reducing the feminine image to a mere body in motion, featuring their butts or their overall nudity as a background for their groundbreaking international videos.

These facts demonstrated for me that these Hip-Hoppers had little or no knowledge of how hard their grandmothers and great-grandmothers struggled to gain the least bit of respect as human beings. Now we have an art form that Super Egos have presented and promoted to destroy the social gains (especially dignity) of the past five hundred years, in exchange for monetary gain and downplayed social recognition. However, it is not the rapper's faults.

Apparently, the adult factor in their lives had failed them. Their mothers and fathers had negated their own historic responsibility to their children. These children have clearly been neglected. They feel as if they have arrived and have a secure and solid social foundation from which to exist, but much to the contrary is true. Hip Hop provides a forum to expose that neglect.

The true spirit of God (Creator of all things) lasts forever and man cannot compete with this. Man must go back to being a child of Creation.

The greatest of all abuses is to deny a child love. It is the parent's responsibility to give and to expose a child to love. Not with toys and material things, but by spending quality time, teaching spiritual values and teaching children how to apply those values to their minds and bodies, as well as by teaching children how to manipulate and to survive within their environment and how, most of all, to be independent of negative influences.

Children are innocent and impressionable when they enter the world. All adults should be committed to teaching all the right things. Love must be shown and felt. It is a vibration that cannot be placed into words.

A child should be able to function and to survive by the age of twelve. Twelve years is a long time to be anywhere and not know how to manipulate and to survive there. Instead, most children are confused. Their natural biological and psychological bodily functions are changing, yet they are confined to the indoctrination of a selfish controlling, egotistical society. Their bodies are telling them something opposite. There is no reason for this diabolical attack except control.

The super egos care about nothing but themselves so it is easy for them to attack, in hopes of controlling, children while they are young, innocent and impressionable.

Children should be given a good, sound, loving and spiritual foundation as soon as they begin to understand their immediate environment. Their parents should be teaching them the truth about their bodies and about how they were conceived and arrived on Earth. Not lies and tall tales, as if some big bird literally brought them here wrapped in a blanket. These ridiculous stories are the beginning of the children becoming liars and liars they will be.

Parents lie to these impressionable minds about their bodies, casting dark shadows over certain parts of the child's body because the super ego has labeled these parts sexual organs. Children's body parts are not sexual organs; they are simply parts of the most magnificent machine in creation.

The human body is one of the most wonderful and beautiful parts of creation, and this should be taught. To separate and to devalue the body is extremely egotistical. To value one part of the body over another is the mission of the ego. The body is one function made-up of many organs and, when it operates in vibration with nature, according to its natural function, it is one magnificent experience.

Appreciation, love and respect are what children should have for the human body, and for that which is truly responsible for it. Parents should teach their children that they (parents) are simply the vessel, used by Creation, to bring another human life into this world. In this way of teaching, children are allowed to make the connection with self and with nature. This approach would allow, enhance and promote love and respect for the total embodiment of Creation (which is God) that is responsible for the child's presence here on Earth.

To give a child the truth is the greatest gift a parent can give. Truth is absolute and is an expression of unconditional love. Truth allows a child to be free within the Oneness of Nature and Creation. This direction prevents the child from ever becoming subject to the ego of another man or to his own ego. You know by now that the Super Ego will never allow sharing to occur.

The super ego must continue to pass laws and to make rules that are designed to prevent the human child from ever entering upon the path to truth. Self thought, autonomy and self-reliance, supported only by the divine spiritual vibration is absolutely what the ego will not allow.

It has often been said that children have a special bond with what has been considered lower-classed animals. Children are also being taught that they are to rule over animals. This is one of the early social games designed to break down the natural process of oneness. Children are taught to believe that they are high-classed animals, thus rulers of Nature, and that they were created to protect and to take care of animals all while watching movies wherein dogs and other animals are protecting and taking care of the humans.

Moreover, our children are taught that they cannot think or reason. What is most ironic here is that they are also being told these same lies about other children of different races, different nationalities and the children of different social economic classes, which is evidence of just how consistent and committed to its mission to control, using separation and devaluing, that the ego is.

Yes, children have a bond with what are considered lower-class animals if for no other reason than because the children are innocent and have yet to be completely polluted by the ego. They have yet to be screwed-up.

The more material the foundation of raising or indoctrination of our children into this civilized, oppressive society, the less spiritual they become.

Parents are the programmers of their children; whether the individual parent or parents at large (it takes a village to raise a child). Parents cut off the true natural spiritual energy of the child, utilizing the belief that they are preparing them (children) for social survival, knowing or not knowing that only a few of these offspring will survive. Why? Because they do not truly survive. Most of these parents are in fact ignorant that they are culpable in their children's destruction.

Moreover, these parents, though many of them have tried, will be told that they did not try, at least not hard enough because their children were exposed to poverty and to other hardships, social conditions promoted by the super ego. We know that these conditions affect a child's natural spiritual content and that these conditions support and sustain the manifestation of ego.

The condition of lesser ego, in the parenting factor, is carried over to the child for the most part. This program is called choosing "the lesser of the two evils." The more naturally spiritual any particular group is the more effectively and persistently is the need to apply this process of control (enslavement).

The Super ego used this process for generations and it still works. Taunting humanity with things needed and promised, though the super ego never intended to share with ordinary humans, or to allow the human to obtain the objects of their desire. This torture, disappointment and anguish became a demonic force within the deprived and the denied human.

The society in which we live, internationally, will never have enough jobs, food, housing, etc, because the super ego has taken us away from our natural selves into an order that it controls, an order in which it allows only a few the benefits of success, reserved only for those who believe in and who are committed to its system. If you straddle the fence, you will suffer and you will fall short, believing that you did not work, pray or believe hard enough.

Master Ego –The Controller

Super Ego – Controlling

Lesser Ego – The Used

The ego separated itself from the natural spiritual order and planted itself in the midst of the garden of the human mind, via taunting and temptation, creating curiosity, and curiosity killed the spirit. Satisfaction will bring it back.

Fornication

Fornication is to penetrate the natural order of creation, motivated by the desires to conquer and to control, to violate the natural order without the spirit of love and oneness. It is the act of abusing another for one's own selfish gratification. In fact you will discover, by closely reading this section, my belief is that any action, exchange or engagement between human beings lacking spiritual substance or a spiritually loving connection is an act of fornication, thus abuse.

Fornication is the unforgivably intentional act of penetration or infiltration of the natural order of Creation for one's own selfish benefit or control, a selfishness devoid of true love and any semblance of oneness while love is the most powerful force in the universe. It is the center of everything. In order to do anything successfully, one must love doing it.

Natural will is the God presence that was destroyed by man's intellectual system. Life is simple. Man over-rationalizes it, causing confusion and destruction. Man is always looking for a way to control, absolutely.

Since the beginning of knowledge, man has been trying to control nature, both internally and externally. Despite his many dubious attempts, to date, he has failed. Yet, he has make progress in certain areas. For instance, early in the 8th and 9th centuries CE, there were men who possessed the will and the energy of the Super Ego who devised an obscure yet diabolical program that they executed. Although this was not the Super Ego's first attempt to control that which is natural, this has clearly been its most effective undertaking. That diabolical program is called "intellect," a program that allows humans to rationalize and to reason with God and with the natural order of Creation.

Going forward, the objective of intellect is to break and to disconnect the human being from the direct influence of his free creative will, the loving will that is naturally a part of each human at its very conception. This natural spiritual vibration, direction and awareness are often referred to as "our first mind" or the sub-mind, which allows the human a simple understanding and acceptance of nature and creation. This application to and appreciation of creation is void the desire to control or to change the natural order. However, intellect is a selfish energy.

Intellect acts to empower those humans who have been exposed and who are learned in the art of social manipulation. The ability to use words to identify feelings desires, and emotions. These words and meaning derive from selfish men with selfish agendas. At the beginning of this intellectual campaign, there were very few who were allowed the egotistical privileges of learning. Moreover, those who were committed and who became fluent or who reached a level of excellence were given awards and special social privileges while the masses were deprived and forced to go without. Once the humans became intellectually astute, they no longer depended on or followed the divine will or direction of our loving Creator. This ego-driven intellectual mind, then, can only rationalize for its own selfish end and needs, for the system that programmed it, with little or no regard for nature, for creation or for any naturally healthy human life.

This intellectual program developed into a campaign that was designed to be and that has been promoted through and by the churches. This was the most diabolical impairment of the human mind. This act of fornication, in which people's minds are intentionally controlled by secular influences and the disingenuous energetic attacks of the Super Ego, allegedly for the individual's own good, is unforgivable.

All humans should have an unconditional love for creation and nature, just as nature and creation unconditionally loves humans. Consider that nature provides us with all that we want, need or desire.

This human – nature union forms the perfect marriage, the most absolute and committed marriage as it was intended, by the Creator, to be. Man and nature. This commitment last forever, even after the death of the physical body, and nothing should cloud, interfere with or violate that bond. In fact, all of the creatures in Creation honor and respect their marriage bond with nature with the exception of the human being. Collectively, humanity respects and honors nothing, not even his fellow man. Not even his self.

This fornication called intellect, then, is one of the most heinously penetrating violations. Man has thus committed adultery, having fled from his Creator-sanctioned commitment with nature, a violation and a sin that cannot be forgiven. Man must correct the actions of this awful act himself.

First, the human must reconnect with the vibrations of creation and allow self to receive the right information and direction.

FORNICATION VERSES MATING

The word fornication carries an obscure and deceptive energy with it. This is a sophisticated intellectual way of saying rape. It is a metaphor for the most spiritual ritual in creation, mating. This ritual is for the extension of life and humanity on Earth.

Mating occurs when man and woman come together and enter each other's body, soul and spirit, in order to bring forth more life. This erotic, pleasurable ritual should always be held sacred, whether new life is produced or not.

Fornication is of the flesh, which cares nothing for the loving spirit. Fornication is motivated by artificial social energy and by the understanding that you-must-do-something-to-get-something mind set. Artificial social energy is a manipulation of the mind and, for many who subscribe to this game, there is a toll extracted.

For it was written, in the Old Testament, that it is better for man to spill his seed in the belly of a whore than to waste it on the ground. Man should never lose focus on the power, importance and sacredness of sperm. If he does, he diminishes his own quality of life.

Yes, there is a toll extracted for having played. The negative energy that promotes and supports the acts of fornication has a direct negative impact on the procreative process. I know that many will question and will argue this point, but I have observed this phenomenon within my own family.

A child born to parents who are involved in a truly spiritual commitment, if for no longer than at the point where in the child is conceived, is a more loving and balanced child. I have also observed children conceived amid hateful and competitive sexual relationships and today's society is filled with them.

Love is a mustard seed that can move mountains. Can you imagine if you could get a basketball's worth of love? The ego only promotes and produces ego while love supports everything and only produces more love.

Fornication is rape of the mind and the body, and any act that takes from nature for the sake of selfishness, without the

Spirit of a loving Oneness, is rape.

Mating is when two physical or biological forces move to the center of their existences, directed by a celestial, invisible, mysterious vibration, creating a spiritual force field. When they meet at the center core of life, this immaculate, spiritual, frictional process causes a spiritual presence and condition that explodes more powerfully than life itself – it creates more life. When a man physically penetrates a woman they are spiritually bonded, which constitutes marriage.

There are four open channels on the human body that aid and support the procreation process: the mouth, nose, anus, and vagina. All four provide the human the potential for immense pleasure in our everyday lives. Without them, we could not live as pleasant and comfortable a life. The procreation process would not properly work if these organs did not work.

Moreover, these four channels are directly connected to the procreative process, with the mouth providing food, communication, oxygen, the elimination of mucus, carbon dioxide and other substances considered waste that the body rejects. The nose provides air and oxygen, the elimination of carbon dioxide and mucus. The anus enables the body to excrete toxins from the body. The vagina receives sperm and eliminates waste.

The Ego's Technological Advancements

The year was 1957, I recall, when my father bought a '57 red and white station wagon. I was 12-years old and eager to be exposed and to learn things outside of my immediate environment. I knew, even then, that the new car would aide me in my mission of discovery. My father later bought a television, too.

We often traveled across the state of South Carolina, he and I, which allowed me to see, first hand, some of the things I had seen on television. My father was also an outdoorsman, so we did a lot of hunting and fishing. Often, he and I would cook our game and eat it in the forest, right where we had caught it and we would get our water from a local stream or spring, fresh water innocents of pollutants and toxins. Sometimes I felt as if I was in the Garden of Eden. As time passed, however, these idealistic conditions changed.

The water in the streams and lakes became polluted. These changes came subject to technological advancements and, whenever I happen to reflect upon early existence, I realize how much technological advancement there were back then. Granted, not everyone I met had a car or even a television, but the fact remains that technological advancement, even when contrasted with the previous century, had occurred. When I compare what we had to what my grandparents had, the differences are monumental.

Being the spiritually founded person I am, I cannot help but to realize the disproportion in economics and in lifestyle of those less fortunate, regardless of their ethnicity. Poor is poor. Thousands are subjected to legislated poverty while the rich and chosen few have everything. Moreover, because the rich have everything, they want more, with no consideration for the poor, the many souls who are dependent on the natural order of Creation to supply their basic day-to-day sustenance.

Therefore, this technological mission continues depriving the poor of food and water, those things supplied by nature and used for millions of years by humans and by other creatures in order to stay alive. What is worse, the pioneers of this devious mission had knowledge of what had happened to civilizations in the past, those that had followed that same path of destruction. However, it did not matter. This zealous, unscrupulous, egotistically driven ambition to destroy the natural resources in this country had to be achieved. So, millions of dollars were invested in all kinds of technological research like space exploration, programs used to control outer space and to check God out to whether He was ready to make a deal. Meanwhile our home planet, Earth, is being polluted with all manner of toxins. Always keep in mind, the Super Egos care only about their selfish mission.

I feel that 1957 was a good time in our history and that we had achieved enough technological advancement. No, we did not have cellular telephones with in-built computers, we did not have cable TV or the internet, but we did have machines that I feel were sufficient for use in communicating around the world. We had airplanes for the air and ships for the ocean. Granted, none of the machines that existed in 1957 was as fast or as sophisticated as they are today, but I think they would have sufficed.

Stop and think for a moment of the billions and billions of dollars that have been poured into the various space programs while over two thirds or more of the people on Earth have not have decent housing, educational opportunities, nutritious food, quality healthcare, or the right to vote. Do not stop thinking, though.

Try to imagine what could have been done with the time, the effort and the money utilized in the space programs if those collective efforts had been channeled in the direction of affecting positive change in the lives of all the impoverished peoples around the world. Even if the space-happy Super

Egos had invested in housing and in decent roads for all of the countries in the world. We would all be working to this day, with no time for war, for manipulating or killing each other in the name of greed and control. We would be working together to make the world a better place for all and making the world a better place for those who will come after us, generation after generation.

Yes, in 1957 people were much happier and contented than are people of today. While it is true that those people were subject to all kinds of prejudices, bigotry, unjustifiable and often undocumented homicides, adjunct poverty, and scant educational opportunity, most of them were content with what they knew: how to create and provide for a family. Today's population cannot begin to imagine how happy the people of 1957 would have been if given the opportunity to work for the betterment of their brothers and their sisters around the world.

However, the mission of love that the people of 1957 were spiritually capable of completing, for the improvement of their fellow human beings, requires love and that is something of which the Super Egos have always been afraid. Love is the social healer and selfishness is the social divider. Selfishness is the ego's foundation.

I know that some may think I do not appreciate advanced technology. Quite the contrary is true. I just believe that enough is enough. If nothing else, we must learn when to hold'em and when to fold 'em. I believe that 1957 was the era wherein we had enough to work with, especially if we were working for the equality and the betterment of all of humanity.

Since 1957, technological advancements have created more negative than positive conditions for the masses. Everything in creation is pollution, the rain forest is dying, many species have gone extinct and the ozone layer is severely compromised. What a price we have paid for technological advancement. Our youth are becoming idiots with little or no respect for common sense as their brains become ever more paralyzed by their reliance on computers to perform simple everyday functions. Today's young people, some of whom I have actually spoken with, have been led to believe that as long as they learn to manipulate a computer they are not required to think.

As much as I know this artificial, computerized technological world is intriguing and enchanting, Creation is being destroyed and technological advancement and reliance have become our demons.

Ego and Terror

Terror is an act of retaliation from having being abused. Abuse is an act whereby someone or something that is innocent and defenseless is willfully violated, unjustly interfered with or destroyed. War and terror occur when those who have been abused retaliate.

Disarm. Why? Because the abuser has everything and the abused nothing. Yet, if the abused disarms, will the abuser return equal share of what has been taken? Oh, we must overlook the lives and the minds that have been destroyed. If not, there will never be true peace. There will never be true disarmament.

What was achieved with the invention of man-killing arms? Ask this question, with fairness, and many questions will be answered.

The Need

For years, men and women have argued and have discussed the need for each other. Does man need woman or the opposite? Man does not need woman, specifically. He needs love. So does woman.

Man and woman are a natural axis. They will be connected whether true love is involved or not.

Love is the vibration to which they really need to connect. It was love from which they came, and to love they must return.

Humans must develop a feel for this vibration we call love and learn to distinguish it from those pangs known as want and desire. Love is also not exclusive to humans. This feeling the need for love can come from any living part of creation. The need for love is the human's first step back to its loving Oneness.

This vibration we have labeled love was tampered with and was interfered with by the intervention of the ego.

The Greatest Gift

The greatest gift a human can give to humanity is his attempt to bring people from all lifestyles together, no matter what race, creed, color, or ethnicity, subject only to the vibrations of love and unity.

Michael Jackson made that attempt. In addition, he was successful.

Just Hurt

Had my share of headaches, toothaches,

Those horny, corny toe aches.

But there is no hurt like heart break,

And there is no hurt like losing the one you love ache.

You just hurt. And just hurt.

No doctor can help you,

No medicine can heal you,

There is no prescription

For love and affection.

You just hurt. And just hurt.

Deep down inside

You hurt a thousand times a thousand times.

You just hurt. And just hurt.

Had my share.

Altering the Human Mind

Questions exploring the origins of life on Earth have always been asked, for example if Creation was this beautiful, tranquil paradise, what happened and why doesn't the beauty still exists? I believe the answers are obvious. They are all around us. The daily action of the human being does not lie. It is my opinion that man is what, in part, he has always been, a creature of Creation. And Creation began once that one entity left that unconditional loving order of Creation. All who submitted and who followed that energy were named and labeled. Even everything a person said did or thought. The very same thing he does today, labeling, and you know what you are. Moreover, you know your own thoughts. How you feel. You could care less whether another is right or wrong, but you had better make the adjustments or you will not survive.

What I have found most interesting is that the animals in the wild do quite well. I mean not the ones man has already names and defined. I mean the ones he is now discovering and those that he has not as of yet. They have survived quite well without the egotistical man. Like always, though, the Ego has something better to offer than the natural order of love. Whenever a human is consumed with wonder, with doubt or with desire, he is a prime candidate to be controlled by the Ego. Wherever you desire to go, the ego will take you there. "But be careful of what you ask for."

The ego prefers choosing only because it was the only entity to go against the loving order. Choice is not a good thing. Why? Because you are always choosing and always restless. You are never satisfied. With each choice you derive a thrill and thrills, for the most part, are life threatening. Yet, man continues this thrill-seeking mission until today.

In the loving order, there is no need for thrills. Everything relies on everything else, just as one into one leaves nothing. If we are sharing equally with each other, it is nothing. Just nothing. However, when the game is not being played fairly, we notice the shortages and the ego does not know how to be fair. When the thrill is over, it needs love, whether win or lose, right or wrong. Unfortunately, the human is hooked on thrills, thrills that will ultimately destroy him. The average human is so inextricably consumed by the influence of the Ego that it is almost impossible for him to recognize that he creates his own destruction. The human has fallen so far away from the loving spiritual entity it was created to be.

Man tested the waters, as he does today, and whenever we take chances we get a thrill, a thrill that the true spirit of love and oneness does not allow, but a thrill that man is hooked on receiving until this day. Now, what happens when the thrill is gone? Man then wants to go back to love, peace and tranquility.

The first big thrill was disconnecting self from the whole and oneness of love. Today, man on every level of life believes he can do it all by himself. After countless failures, man continues to try to make it happen. He is hooked on the thrill.

Thrill seeking has taken many lives and has destroyed countless empires. As always, when the thrill is gone, man's single most desires are love, peace and tranquility. But he never truly finds them because his preference is the big thrill. Man tried endlessly to find what is on the other side of love, peace and tranquility. His ego will never allow him to accept the truth: that his thrill-seeking choices can only afford him disaster, destruction, confusion, and eternal turmoil. And, as long as the human Super Ego is committed to this way of thinking he, the lesser human ego, will always be subject to these condition, the same conditions, in fact, that we are living today; trying to solve problems by creating newer sets of problems with man as the biggest problem of all.

The original big thrill came from taking the chance from defecting from the loving universal

Oneness to self-reliance and selfishness, then forcing this change, for the sake of selfish control. The suffering masses of the world are combating these very same conditions every day. The Super Egos will not come together in universal harmony. They are all motivated by fear and the same selfish energies: greed and the thrill of conquering.

What the world needs today is a universal campaign, based on a committed universal loving Oneness and harmony.

<u>Psychological Warfare</u>

My story about Vietnam is about trust, honor and respect.

I was a young Black American in 1965, full of ideas, and complete with a southern Christian foundation. At that time, I had no reservations about or objections to the idea of serving my country. In this, I was similar to many young men of my era. My father and the uncles on both sides of my family had enlisted into the armed services, and had fought either during the Korean occupation or in World War II. Therefore, entering the service was not something I feared. However, I did not know that there was going to be a war. I was drafted into the army in June 1965, and completed my basic training at Fort Jackson, South Carolina, AIT.

In AIT, I was trained to function as a radio operator. Near the end of my AIT training, we began jungle warfare training. I still had no idea that I was about to be sent to war. My superiors informed me that I was scheduled to transfer to Georgia, in September 1965, to receive advanced radio communication training. I never got there.

I was packed and prepared to leave base that September day, the one I was scheduled to depart en route to Georgia. Immediately before loading the bus, however, we received orders indicating that our country was engaged in a war being waged in a place I had never heard of: Vietnam. A Captain briefed us that morning, explaining that our group was scheduled to leave for Fort Ord, CA, to received advanced jungle warfare training. Again, I never got there.

One hour after arriving at California's Travis Air Force Base, my group was commanded to change our uniforms, which we did promptly. It was then that we were informed that we were actually on our way to Vietnam. My stress level elevated perceptively.

Upon arrival in Vietnam, our group received small arms fire from the ground. There were men of our group who fell completely apart at the sounds of the gunfire, at the reality that we were in an active warzone. We continued exiting the plane.

It was one week after I arrived in Vietnam when an American man, who identified himself as an ex-sergeant, approached me and explained that he had defected from the American army and had joined the Vietcong. He further told me that America was wrong for being in Vietnam and that his people would pay me the equivalent of $75.00 American currency a week, also providing me with a safe place to live, if I too defected. The man said he would return to me, in the same place we had met up, the following day in order to receive my answer. I, along with two of my friends, expressed our disinterest.

It was during my second week in Vietnam that I received orders to report to MACV Headquarters. Once there, I was informed that I had been assigned to MACV. A few soldiers and I received a four-day orientation, within a padded and soundproofed room. The man proctoring the orientation was code-named "Mr. Ed." He said he had been sent to Vietnam, from the Pentagon, and that the information he was supplying us with was highly confidential.

Mr. Ed. gave us the dos and don'ts. We were exposed to all operations, then underway, supporting the US Army, the Vietcong and the North Vietnamese regulars. After, on a large movie screen, we were shown pictures of the lead commanders of both the North Vietnamese and of the Vietcong armies. Later, Mr. Ed detailed the meaning of psychological warfare.

According to Mr. Ed, psychological warfare included the images we were shown, including those of soldiers who bodies had been ravished by the wildlife as well as by the Vietnamese enemy, bodies of American men who penises had been severed and were shoved into their mouths. Mr. Ed explained, while the desecrated body was still on the screen, that this particular tactic was readily employed by the Communists and that it proved very effective in dissuading the local villagers from supporting the American Army.

We were also told that any Vietcong we encountered would more than likely prove to be Vietnamese regular as soon as we turned our backs on them. We were told that we could not trust the Vietnamese as a whole. Yet, we heard, during that same orientation, that we would have to place at least one Vietnamese nearby wherever an American was working because, as a force for good, we did not want to give the local citizens the impression that we were trying to take their country from them.

We learned that we would not be allowed to carry any weapons into the cities of Vietnam, unless we were on guard duty, and that we were not allowed to shoot at the Vietnamese unless fired upon first. However, we were told, if we had a small weapon, we could carry it, undetected, inside of a brown paper bag, provided it remained undetectable. If it were discovered, we would be on our own. Moreover, Mr. Ed explained that if we killed a Vietnamese within a city's limits, and were caught, we would be jailed and tried within Vietnam. However, if found guilty of murder, we would be extradited back to the United States.

By the end of the fourth day, I was thoroughly frustrated. It was then that I was informed I had been attached to an advisory team, the Me Kong Delta, where I would function as a trainer of the South Vietnamese soldiers. I was told that, once in the position, my head would be worth $500. I also learned that, until further notice, I would work for and receive my orders from MACV.

During the weeks following my MACV orientation, I was subject to the myriad of stresses anyone could imagine, being in an active warzone, clear across the world from the place and anyone I knew, without an assigned weapon. While working at MACV and awaiting the day I would be ordered to fulfill the responsibilities of Advisor, which would place a $500 bounty on my head, I witnessed a large portion of my headquarters being blown-up. The sergeant who had informed me that I was assigned to the Advisory Team, in fact, was one of the men killed during the explosion. Upon searching, we discovered rubber band wrapped hand grenades placed within the tanks atop the commodes within the latrines. Stress? There was a lot of stress. I would also witness, during my time in Vietnam, a hotel explosion and the incendiary destruction of one of the eateries I would frequent, known by my friends and I as the Floating Restaurant.

Two weeks after my briefing at MACV, I fell asleep in a rickshaw, at the end of a night on the town, and awoke to discover myself deep within the jungle. My only weapon was a pocketknife. I pressed my knife to the driver's neck, which helped him to understand my intentions, as I pointed in the direction of the town from which he had carried. He quickly righted his course.

While assigned to MACV Headquarters, I lived at the Maricord Hotel. There was a 50-caliber gun within a bunker directly beneath my bedroom window. The gunner was scared most of the time, we were the rest of us, but especially so at night. He was always shooting something, a rat or anything else that moved, and this happened repeatedly throughout the night. Looking from my hotel window at night, the countryside would light-up as bright as daytime, as there were many weapons being fired. One night, though, the gunner accidentally shot a Vietnamese man.

I was given a postal position, while attached to MACV, at the Tan Son Nhut Air Base. The post office was actually located within an airplane hangar. The Vietcong would drop pamphlets proclaiming their intentions to blow-up the air base. Every time these threats occurred, which was not infrequently, the Air Force would leave the base, turning responsibility for it over to the Army personnel. Which meant me.

The army personnel would scour the hangar for mines and any other explosive, using sticks to probe trashcans and other dark places. Sometimes I was left alone to check for bombs. One day, on my way to work, while traveling in a six-truck convoy, some Vietnamese children tossed grenades into the last two trucks. I was riding in the second truck from the front of the convoy. Moreover, I was then assigned to pack and to prepare the bodies of the dead American soldiers for shipment back to the United States.

While in Vietnam, I began to experience recurring nightmares. In one dream, I was inside of red velvet-lined coffin, suffering, trying to escape it. This dream was very real to me and, upon awakening, I could feel the pressure points caused from being confined within that small space. I still have that dream to this day.

Although I was in Vietnam for a short while, my experiences are my experiences and they will be with me for the rest of my life. I volunteered to fight and to die for my country. The Vietnam War was waged in a foreign place and I could have died at any time while there. I was in Vietnam from November 1965 until January 1966, during a time when most major conflicts occurred within the cities.

It has been estimated that, during the time I was in-country, Americans were killing approximately 75-Vietnamese a day on the country roads, simply running the Vietnamese down with trucks, which is a far greater number than what was reported, as having died while engaged in jungle combat, back in the United States. However, most of the Americans were killed on the city streets: whorehouses, restaurants and hotels. While I was in Saigon, several soldiers were killed in a place called Hundred Pea Alley.

While at a Saigon nightclub one evening, I witnessed an American sergeant beat an American soldier to the floor. The sergeant then kicked and stomped the younger man, repeatedly. After the massacre ended, I learned that the vicious beating had occurred because the sergeant saw the young soldier crying and investigated. It was after learning that the youth openly wept because he had just learned his older brother had fallen victim to the enemy, been captured, been decapitated, and been dragged through the streets that the sergeant responded with the beating. By the final days of 1965, though, it was the plight of my own family that weighed heavily on my mind.

I learned, in December 1965, that my mother had taken sick which left me as the sole supporter of my seven sisters and brothers. My family made an official request for my return home. My captain, however, refused to send me. Instead, he sent me to the chaplain. "Chappie" explained to me the fact that America was at war (as if I did not know), that my fellow soldiers needed me to stay in Vietnam and help them to fight and that the Vietnamese were all heathens who could never be trusted to do that which is right because they did not believe in our God. Ironic that now, 30-years after the end of the American occupation in Vietnam, that these same people own a number of the businesses in my neighborhood today. Chappie further explained that I had done more than enough for my family, having enlisted into the armed services, and that the time had arrived for me to do something for my country. In essence, Chappie agreed with my captain. However, my family was successful in negotiating my discharge.

Two weeks before leaving Vietnam, I was finally issued a weapon and ammunition. I never got the chance to use my service-issue weapon in Vietnam due to the political strings my family was able to pull. I was discharged from the army with a claim of hardship. Nevertheless, that was not the end of my Vietnam hell.

Before leaving, I was given a security orientation. I was then told to report to Cobra compound in Saigon, where I learned that is I ever disclosed any of the information I had been exposed to while in-county, I would be fined $10,000 and receive a 10-year imprisonment.

For many years, following my return to the United States, I refused to talk about Vietnam, not sure what might be considered confidential. Even now, I find myself reluctant to talk about Vietnam with certain people, mostly those I do not know well.

Vietnam is one of those nightmarish experiences from which you never fully awake. I certainly grew-up while there. It is the place I learned, in short order, not to trust anyone or anything, and the place I learned never to travel to the same destination via the same route.

But to carry, in confidence, all of the things I'd been exposed to in Vietnam for so many years only to discover, gradually, that the entire soldier experience was predicated on a big games played by politicians, a game that caused the deaths of so many, is tragic. It was stressful then and it remains stressful now.

PFC George L. Dunbar

The Ego and Man

The diabolical, invisible force that fuels this system is called ego. The ego does not belong to the body and the body does not belong to it. The ego can only influence the spiritually weak and affect those who have a desire for its possessions. The ego is an energy that derived from the friction of resisting the direction of the true loving God.

All of creation is supposed to be free, to exist subject to only the laws of nature. Man has taken that right away from life. Man only allows freedom, a process that allows creation to exist only for the selfish needs and wants of the Super Egos (the men who are in control). That part of Creation man does not understand and, unfortunately, what he does not want man destroys.

Ego means the eradication-of-God. Ego is an invisible, obscure, negative energy that is manifested during a deprivation process. For instance, when a human is deprived of the right to live in harmony with the true and loving, unselfish God, in harmony with the spirit of Oneness. It has be said that this manner of deprivation consumes the average human being by the time they are 12-years old, after which time, the human starts a journey of competitiveness, selfishness and greed. This quest has one central goal: never to be in a state of deprivation again and so the person's actions are justified with each conquest they achieve, in the name of an artificial and egotistical god.

The ego is the greatest of all liars. First, it tells you that you are it and that it is you. It manipulates the flesh, meaning the entire human body, including the brain, which promotes negative thoughts and confusion. In the world of Henry David Thoreau, this process is aptly referred to as "creating a problem to solve a problem."

The ego has its own thought system called "intellect." This system allows the human being the right to rationalize God and Creation. The ego will not allow the loving vibration of Nature to enter the human mind. It has an invisible shield called intellect to prevent the natural vibration from entering. The natural will and vibration of Creation means little or nothing to the ego of man. The ego makes no sense to love, and the ego will not share Creation in the spirit of Oneness.

This egotistical process started with a campaign called civilization. Some selfish men decided they had the right way for all humans to live, and they were diabolically committed to carrying-out their plan by whatever means were necessary. This process has been repeated throughout the Earth and it is still being utilized today. This method of suppression and deprivation creates a force of negative resistance called "ego." Just imagine forcing a large spring into a small box. Eventually, the spring is going to free itself and do some damage to the box. That damage is being done to civilization right now. Destruction and confusion are everywhere.

Every child has a mind of its own, every man has selfish dreams and the world is in turmoil. The Ego caused these conditions and, by way of mass media, the Super Egos inform us, daily, that they do not intend to fix it. Believe it if you wish.

Never forget my understanding of ego: it solves problems by creating other problems.

What We Are Not Allowed

We are not allowed our own spiritual autonomy. Why not? Because the super ego human mind set has robbed us of it, with its selfish, intellectual, civilized campaign and it is obscure socially, economically and politically manipulative systems, systems that will leave you in the middle of an ocean of man-eating sharks, in a canoe without a paddle, provided you do not adhere to its direction.

Unfortunately, this is the only time the human divorces himself from the ego and makes the turn towards the loving Oneness of Creation.

Bad Blood

It is my belief that hostile energy can be passed down from generation to generation. Some energy is more hostile than others are. What determines which energy is most hostile is the depth of a family's committed obsession to intense negativity, energy that is only focused on promoting separation, destruction, control, and deception? Over time, this negative energy forma s double force in the body of the human. Psychologist of the 19th Century identified this apparation-esque double and named it Doppelganger.

Throughout history, the energy of the Doppelganger (an extension of the human ego) has been given many other names and I myself refer to it as the false spiritual manifestation of the ego. What I find interesting, after having studied the writings on Doppelgangers and having spoken to people over the years on this topic, is that, more than not, the Doppelganger energy is often confused for being the natural loving spirit of God. Though the movement and motion of this energy runs parallel with the true natural spirit of God, the Doppelganger has a separatist and selfish nature; it would rather be on its own, independent of the loving spirit of oneness.

Fortunately it cannot be. Why? The Ego has no life source of its own, so it is 100% dependent upon the loving spirit of God. Love supports the ego's every motion and movement. That is its nature. In fact, love supports everything that has life or that appears to have life (think of the wind).

Because of the ego's dependence on natural life, the source of which it cannot control, the ego forged and welds another weapon in its vain attack on the spirit of God called deception. This weapon serves to convince the human being that it (Ego) is more powerful than the true loving God is, even though its power and autonomy lie solely within the realm of the material world of imitation.

In as much as the ego has tried to control all of creation and has not, it remains forever committed to its mission and it will direct every human being that submits to its direction to a point of disaster and self-destruction. After guiding the human to his own social, political, or familial death, the ego will leave. In fact, the ego flees from its human host shortly before the human being's actually physical death because it (ego) fears the death of its host, having no life source of its own.

Humans that are more committed to and consumed with the negative energy of the ego are known herein as the Super Egos. Although there are different levels within the ego structure, most humans never achieve the depth of negative saturation required to be considered a Super Ego, so they remain the lesser ego. Though lesser egos, many human beings, having forgotten how to and why they should connect to the true loving spirit of Oneness, are confused and confusedly accept that the accoutrement of the Super Egos are worth acquiring.

Those of the lesser egos desire to become like the Super Ego as evidenced by their (lesser ego) attempts to dress, to live and to acquire as many toys as they believe are owned by the Super Egos—cell phones, computers, televisions, automobiles, ridiculously stylish clothing, diamonds, etc.

This stressful and negative egotistical journey away from true selfhood (Oneness) affects the genetic bank within the human being and the negativity is passed down through the bloodline. A negative energy, once unleashed, cannot be controlled or directed by a human only because the choice to accept the negative was made generations ago. "Seed of your seed."

No one knows where negative energy will manifest itself or when. The ego is effective in its mission because it is capricious. It has all of the natural, loving, spiritual characteristics and abilities except one. The ego cannot give life. Yet, it is obscure, seductive and convincingly deceptive approach is easily accepted by the human as being the source of life. The reason this deceptions works is because human beings are selfish and the ego affords them the source for justifying their selfishness.

Once the negative energy is accepted and cultivated within the human, their seed becomes saturated and, before long, so does the entire human family, causing health issues, mental illness, distrust of loved ones and of self, and this bad blood, this negative and destructive energy spreads.

Because the ego has no true spiritual substance and is very low in self-esteem, it makes everything it touches bow down to it. This is how it supports the lie that it is supreme and thus responsible for all of creation.

In my understanding, the energy of the ego, the energy that desires to rule Creation, came from the stagnation, the control and the state of being in bondage to the ego. The human condition and existence are absolutely controlled and totally influenced by the ego. During innocence is where this conditioning process starts.

We, in our innocence, are taught that we are born in sin and conceived in iniquity, or we learn to live by the social rule of accepting the lesser of the two evils, whereby we surrender all of our natural spiritual feelings and submit to social dictations.

We arrive in this world via a vessel made from flesh and the flesh is what we are taught to respect, being naïve and innocent. Moreover, these falsities are taught to us by the very ones who are supposed to love us the most and by the first humans we know. No choice there. Therefore, our programming begins.

We are quickly introduced to things we do not understand, being given things and having them taken away from us, actions that create in us attitudes of manipulation. Parents then teach us to separate our bodies when they place value on certain parts of us over other parts. These are games and schemes of the ego. This process is so entrenched and intense that our parents never consider that our bodies are mere capsules, only vessels in which we live.

To be fair, though, we can't really blame our parents for these shortcomings because they were programmed by the same process, knowing very little or nothing about the love spirit themselves. They commit themselves to the only thing they do know, which is the flesh. They consistently ignore the natural loving spiritual self.

Then, once the egotistical seed has been planted, and the human becomes aware of self, the once naïve and innocent begins to play the games against those who were responsible for its recent programming, against those who were the teachers. The parents.

At first, parents find the games and schemes their children play cute and funny. They feel that their jobs and responsibilities to their child are being accomplished. It is not until the program becomes an economical problem or a social embarrassment that they find fault in their child. Yet they truly do not understand that they, themselves, are the ones at fault.

What most parents fail to understand is that the negative energy that goes into the procreative process has a direct effect on their offspring. These are some of the ways that demonic energy manifests and sustains itself. In this scenario, the parents are the Super Egos as they have absolute control over the child. The child is the lesser ego. The parents feel they have a social responsibility to control the ego that they have created, to direct it to survive in a world of other egos and to be socially accepted. However, it does not stop there.

Parents have the most difficult job of suppressing the natural will and love spirit, thus creating the demonic energy. This suppression requires the creation of a system of false love, which consists of lies, selection processes, self-denial, segregation, integration of evil, value systems, etc. Moreover, if the parents fail to achieve their desired goal of directing the lesser ego (their child), the environment, outside of the parental tutelage, has much harsher lessons to teach the child.

Some lesser egos are easier to process or to program, depending on how they are conditioned and based on how committed they have been to being accepted within the society in which they live. However, if the parent is more committed to the spirit of love, they will institute a system of choice, affording the child the right to explore a direction for itself.

Always remember, dear parents, that the procreative energy is influenced and infected by the social attitude and commitment of the parent. The suppression of an egotistical energy causes all kinds of negatives. The negatives promote frustration only because the Super Egos refuse to allow the lesser egos equal rights, as long as the Super is responsible for the lesser.

If the lesser ego does not have a way out or an escape valve, it explodes, losing all connection with and consciousness of love. Still, love does not leave the demon. The demon, formerly known herein as the lesser ego, uses love to manipulate and to control other lesser egos. It becomes a tool of separation and of destruction, using everything naïve and innocent in its path.

Fear

Fear is the energy that motivates the conqueror. The potentially conquered always anticipate being conquered or conquering all that is around him, for the fear that some other power (i.e. the power he himself has recently conquered) will one day rise and do the same things to him that he has done to them and to others.

Fear is a universal vibration that keeps all animals, including humans, aware of the consequences faced when going against the forces of love.

The Super Ego of man has gone completely away from true love. Its passion is to force all lesser egos to worship his artificial material world. The Ego's fear of those who do not share its feelings or passions causes it to conquer, destroy, control, and force others to think and to feel as it does. The ego carries out these acts by depriving, starving, destroying, and by cutting off the natural resources that creation has afforded those within the conquered region in order to promote basic human survival there.

When man disconnected himself from universal love, he no longer felt the vibrations or the needs of nature. He is like an out of control machine or a completely undisciplined child, with no foundation and knowing no barriers. Man is lost in his world of selfish wants and desires.

Living out a Word

A word is harmless. Just a combination of letters placed together to define or describe a person, a place or a thing. However, living out a word is different.

I have always found that living out a word was much different from the word's meaning or definition. What I mean by this is that giving practical daily application to a concept (a sound) is not the same as deriving a basic understanding through reading or any other form of tutelage. Practical and daily application to a word is an individual endeavor, based on his or her environment, as well as the response they get from others within that same environment, which differs still from the response an individual's practical and daily application to a word would get from someone raised within a different environment.

All of these human interactions (similar backgrounds and different one) and necessarily different applications form and frame a much different interpretation of a word, of an action, and the different backgrounds from which a word (or action based on one's understanding) derives, often causing confusion. I am repeatedly confronting this confusion while writing this book.

While attempting to address the angst of many within these pages, I have sought spiritually sound and correct wording to reach my readers, in order to provide them with a foundation from which to re-address their own actions and thoughts: seeking solidification, justification and authentification of the words employed herein in many dictionaries, not realizing that I am, in fact, writing about my life experiences. I am writing about my personal application to life as well as my struggles to live out the words and the phrases that I have been given and programmed to use for my success and survival. Who else, I ask myself, is more qualified. If I cannot justify and authenticate my own life than no one can. Within that thought, I realized how much control the Super Ego had over me.

Lawyers, doctors, professor, scientists, archaeologists, anthropologists, and sociologists are just a few of the egos that have been sanctioned and given absolute rights to form and to frame the human experience. These egos dissect and explore the psychological, physiological and biological existence of the human being but with scant consideration of the most important part of human existence: the spirit. The reason so little consideration is given to the human spirit is that the spirit of life cannot be manipulated nor controlled.

The egos that have been sanctioned by the Super Ego have formulated and created scientific processes by which they are said to determine which human beings are superior and which humans are inferior, but they always exclude the spirit of the individual human. They determine potential and have created all manner of machinations to determine an individual's capabilities by exploring the individual's bone structure and genetics. Then the egos define the characteristics and place human beings into social groups and categories, subject to rules, laws and socio-economic limitations.

The most devastating of the limitations imposed by the Super Egos are economical, agricultural and educational. These three acts of deprivation create a completely different understanding of everyday words and phrases. Subject to these conditions, words and phrases just don't mean the same as they would to individuals not subjected to these deprivations, especially in light of the fact that the only reference or foundation for understanding how well one is doing or how well one is progressing is based on the selfish measurements established by the privileged egos. It is only after the Super Egos have ravished, pillaged and conquered the lesser egos, and are controlling most of the world's resources for its own selfish gain, which the conquered realize that their understanding of the words they'd been taught do not coincide with the actions they have witnessed.

For centuries, the Super Egos have carried out these diabolical acts of deprivation for the sake of control, leaving the indigenous conquered masses without the basic resources to survive. The frustration, anger and hatred that develop resulting from extreme deprivation have no end. The "fuck it" and "fuck you" attitudes are formed. These attitudes, over time, prompt new thought processes, new words and new phrases. New understandings and new meanings.

Words carry feelings, sounds and understandings. For instance, if a man is being mistreated, tortured, abused, or totally disrespected, forsaken of the rights given him by God and by the laws of the land, the feeling, the sound and the meaning of words take on another color. Unless you can empathize with his pain, you are unconscious, regardless of how you try to color the situation.

Love and trust are no longer at the apex of the conquered masses' agendas and their words are audible proof. Hate and distrust are formed. The spiritual content of a word is getting over, manipulation and survival by whatever means possible or necessary. This negative attitude is passed down from generation to generation.

If the people of this earth believed in the concepts of one God, 1 love and 1 Creation, then words would have one universal meaning. The single meaning would be based on the vibration of love. Yet, how could this be possible in a world wherein one man (group) takes, by overwhelming force, the food out of the mouth of another man, kills the victim's entire family and destroys his lands. Yet, at the same time, convincing all victims---those fortunate enough to have survived the initial assaults---that the conquering and pillaging are all acts of love and unity. At this point in the game created by the Super Egos, words like love, unity, trust, sharing, and unity take on entirely different meaning for the conquered.

If a man learns the spoken word, language and definitions from a tribe outside of his own, he will never have the true meaning or understanding of himself or the true meaning or understanding of the situation in which he lives. One must live in the culture from whence the word emerged. All men must live out the spoken word of his native tribe for everlasting improvement while he is getting a better understanding of himself.

Most men live their entire lives, never getting a true understanding of self, which means trying to formulate a letter, a sound or a feeling in order to form a single word to represent his personal feeling, which can be a lifelong task. Yet, unfortunately, most never achieve a basic understanding. Not even of self.

Love has one profound foundation and its own means of communication. Hatred, frustration, deprivation, anger, and despair occupy the complete opposite end of the communication spectrum. I guess your own personal meaning for these words depends on which God(s) you worship.

Man's Best Friend is a Dog

A man's best friend is a dog. This statement clearly shows and illustrates what a contradicting liar the ego is. It lies just to hear itself sound good to itself. One would think that man's best friend would be another man. And why not? Well, the ego's number one subject for control is a human. Moreover, the human enjoys his ego for social acceptance and survival, which means he cannot be trusted.

Therefore, this makes a dog more reliable and trustworthy. Even after man tells himself this lie, he cannot ever be truly loyal or committed to the dog. Dogs catch pure hell in man's egotistical world. They are used for selfish pleasures and desires, which often time results in the canine's death.

A dog is man's best friend. A dog has no funerals and he has no churches. A dog has no heaven or hell, no God or minister. Man says dogs have no soul, either. And he is correct. It has none until it is domesticated and trained to respond to the needs of man's ego.

The soul of any animal is its social mind, its social, psychological and intellectual foundation. In short, its ego. Sole. Soul. Both are foundations:

Sole – physical foundation (the feel),

Soul – the spirited minded self

Why can't we just let dogs be dogs for their own sakes and let humans be man's best friend? Because our egos would never allow this.

On Adulthood

I am an adult African American man, whatever that means. Two questions that have often sprung to mind, when someone questions me are, "Which self are you asking" or "What self are you talking to."

Well, I believe that there exists, within all spirituality-minded people, something that I call the baby factor. It is that part of us that we spend our entire lives protecting. The innocence that remains beyond all programs, thus socially unpolluted. The very purity of my being and of my existence. For this reason, I feel I can get an honest answer.

I go into my spiritual closet and begin to ask questions, questions that no one seems to have the answers for or that no one is willing to answer. For instance, man means being responsible and being in control of one's own destiny, and then the American prototype for this "man" is white or is of European decent. They are the ones who seem to be in control of everything in America. That being the case, then, what does "man" mean when it comes to me, as a Black or African American man?

Contrary

The iconography that celebrates and exalts the memorial of all the Super Egos around the world is clear proof of how much the human has forgotten their true loving, creative beginning. These icons were dedicated and erected in order to empower the forces of separation and control. Never dedicated to the loving Oneness. For example, a wounded human body is proof and evidence of what an egoless mind does once it makes the turn back to Oneness. A body that is wounded does not open wider or expand. In its attempt to heal, it struggles desperately to solidify itself.

It is my belief that all that is natural, and of the original creative order, has a spirit. All that goes against the natural order is mere energy. This energy emanates from the resistance and the non-existence of true unconditional love. This rebellious and extremely intense force creates a violent and emotional condition in the midst of creation. From this condition sprang the desire to harness and to control all components of the natural, creative order. The negative campaign is called ego.

In order to harness, for the purpose of control, the natural spirit of Creation is to create negative energy. This energy creates stress, anxiety and all other negative disorders in nature. The conservation of the natural creative order and the appreciation of it is where we find true love. The further the human gets away from the natural order, the more we find ourselves subject to the negative conditions we experience today.

Today, true love and truth are not appreciated. The more we disrespect nature and natural creativity, which is responsible for existence, the more we support the ego and its mission to spread negative energy everywhere.

Carnal is fleshy covering. Away from the Spirit. The Spirit knows the flesh, but the flesh knows not of the Spirit. Everything from the mind to the skin on your body is flesh. To make it simple, a computer may be programmed to respond to electricity, but electricity knows not of the computer.

Everything that is materialistic is made for the flesh, of the flesh and by the flesh. Unfortunately, too, it will destroy the flesh. In order to connect with the Spirit, you must become aware of the Spirit. The ego's responsibility is to keep the human from achieving that awareness.

On Rationalization

How does one rationalize irrational behavior? The attempt to rationalize said behavior is truly a waste of time. This egotistical process goes far back, before the beginning of time. Yet, the personal condition belongs only to the individual. Yet, because the individual cannot see or feel the invasion of this energy, he believes that his actions are creating the conditions in which he lives.

He is left only with thought, to rationalize and to reason about something he knows nothing about, which leads him to a state of confusion, irrational thought and behaviors. Because he cannot find a reason why he would be destroying himself, he must blame someone or something, regardless of the circumstances or consequences. Someone must be held responsible. The end justifies the means. That is all that matters.

The ego never submits to ego. It only submits to love, then immediately runs from it. You see, the ego is capricious. It has no committed foundation. Without love, the ego is alone, all by itself, seeking that weaker prey for its very survival. Ego preys on the weakest soul, taking advantage of it in order to sustain its own survival. Yet, the human still does not know that he is being controlled. He cannot rationalize the irrational and make spiritually sound and loving good sense.

Heaven

The ego has created its own God, named it and given it a home. This home has been given a name: "heaven." It is a place up there or out there or somewhere, but never down there because that is reserved for hell, or is it all merely a state of mind?

What is most interesting about this concept is that God and heaven have most of the characteristics of humans and of the places where humans live, each resembling the value systems prevalent on Earth. God's features and image resemble the ego that created them. The nationality and complexion of God match that of the prevalent political bodies in power when the individual images were created.

Heaven is a place for the lazy, sex-hungry, greedy people of the Earth. It has lots of valuable things, such as diamonds, silver, ivory, and gold, and let us not forget the virgins.

Yet, we are taught that God has no value systems. What is more interesting, it is the Ego's value system that prevents people from living together in Oneness on Earth. Yet, religious people devote and dedicate their lives to continuing this anti-Creation and pro-ego process, dedication that is designed to keep people separate. The one difference is that they---the people who get to Heaven, those sitting amid enormous wealth with nowhere to spend their riches---do not have to work. This is their reward for not standing-up to and confronting the Egotistical system that oppresses, controls and denies them of their own spiritual self.

A child raised in the wild with lions will respond to the behavior of the lion. Yet, the child's biological functions will be that of a human. The child will become aware of his environment but he will be free from intellect, egotistical indoctrination and its influences. The child will learn to survive until the end of its life.

The Ego would deem such existence primitive, bestial and hostile. However, this natural system is more spiritual then our controlling egotistical life. Yet, we call such living animalistic and lower class. How do we judge animals as less than ourselves when their spiritual connection with nature is purely instinctual?

Instinct bespeaks one responding to one's own limitations and conscience. Of course, I am not talking about the mentally impaired. We (society) are well aware that this disorder occurs amid both lower and supreme animals, for whatever reasons.

A lower-class animal must be domesticated, trained, indoctrinated, and completely controlled in order to be accepted and appreciated by the human ego, regardless of how brutal and painful the process of domestication is to the animal. Yet, what is interesting is that this same process of brutalization is used by human beings against other human beings, for the sake of furthering civilization in general.

Beast

The Super Egos have a quest and are committed to conquering and to controlling the natural will and spirit of the true Creator. This will was and is still given to man and to all living creatures within Creation. However, the ego does not intend to allow anyone or any force to halt its quest to conquer all and fornication is the process it uses.

The Super Ego violates by forcing and by penetrating ones' private space. Because the Super Ego has control of its artificial, materialistic world, it carries out these diabolical acts by depriving alleged enemies of the basic means to survive, until the lesser ego submits. At this point, the lesser ego develops the ideal that it must never again be in a deprived state. This idea fosters the "do unto others before they do evil to you" credo, an attitude clearly prevalent today: bad attitudes abound, relationships that are doomed to fail from the onset due to excessive emotional baggage the participants bring; the competition and the distrust inherit in the individual, etc. Moreover, because this "do unto others" attitude is apparent in the people of society, it is also included within the programming and dissemination of information.

Today's dominant face of evil is not witnessed in the actions of humans doing evil directly to others. Super Ego is now placing its evil mind set into machines and that mind set is committing evil against all of humankind. So we have moved beyond Shelley's <u>Frankenstein</u> and Stoker's <u>Dracula</u>. Technology is the dreaded beast of the day.

The beast is a large computer said to be located somewhere in Europe. It is to this specific pile of metal is what human beings, throughout the world, are assimilating.

Man has largely forfeited his spirituality in favor of intellect. Now he is surrendering his humanity to a machine. Both children and adults, the world over, are worshipping machines (computers). The value of human life means nothing anymore. Speed and immediate gratification are the rewards for this loss of humanity, and the applications are limitless: dating, job acquisition, teaching and learning, raising children, etc., all by way of machines.

Yet, if we are to believe that the computer is spiritually right, then natural truth is absurd. Computers are programmed by selfish, materialistic people who input information into the mainframes that is saturated with the selfishness of the society they represent. Therefore, the information provided by the computer is also evil.

Evil and selfishness have consumed our society on every level to the extent that the average human seems completely comfortable within this muck of madness, committing evil and selfish act regularly. They do them to each other with smiles on their faces. Both man and ego truly believe that their self-glorifying actions are acts of love.

For information to be effective enough to influence loving and productive people, it must come from a loving human being. Not a machine. Teaching love requires more than just the utterance of words. The teaching of love induces feelings, expressions and vibrations. None of these a machine can produce. Yet, man is committed to placing machines in areas where humans once taught. A machine that has no feeling, no consideration for soul, spirit or the human factor is set-up to oversee humans.

In order to bring true love back to the human being, it must be shown and expressed for the learners to see and feel. Love is infective and it must become humanity's last infective pandemic.

Evil and selfishness have consumed our society on every level. So much so that the human is comfortable committing evil, selfish acts. They do them to each other with smiles on their faces, believing that theirs are acts of love. The human lesser-deprived ego truly believes that it is love that it gets from the Super Ego. Love is not closed, conditional or selfish.

Love is open, never secretive. Open for everyone to see. Love is a vibration, a feeling. When one attempts to place the feeling into words, the feeling is diminished. Love promotes honesty, unity, oneness and togetherness.

Can society reconcile good with evil and create a loving environment with machines? Well, it is not working and will never work. Love repels evil like the water from a duck's back.

If we would just stop for a second and observe, with a loving and unselfish mind, we would recognize what has happened and what is happening to our children, in light of their relationships with computers.

Today's children spend more time with their machines than they do with their siblings, with their friends and with their parents. They have even killed and will continue to kill in order to obtain these machines. They have and are becoming even more bestial, with no feelings for the human factor or for the spirit of life. Today's children have no respect for the natural order of creation and love is an intangible fantasy.

Under

The human is subject to a system consumed by falsehood, misinformation and lies. The Super Ego has placed a dome over humanity. This dome is called freedom.

Freedom means that you are allowed certain privileges but only after your total indoctrination and domestication within the Super Egos guidelines. You must follow its rules, laws and policies for the remainder of your life, unless you wish to have the privileges revoked. When revoked, you are not able to buy, trade, sell, or work. You may even disappear.

The word under is an obscure and abstract word, especially when it is applied to describing the social processes. It is so well placed and orchestrated in our international communities that most people have no idea that they are under or subject to anything.

Under means, in accord with a popular dictionary: "a low position, inferior, controlled, and even unconsciousness. These definitions help me to understand where society is today. Socially unconscious, sedate and tranquilized by hope and promises. Daily manipulation by socio-economic, political and religious games, games whereby human beings are obscurely directed or outright forced into a state of inadequacies and dependence. They are robbed of self-autonomy and independence.

Most humans never know where this controlling energy is coming from while others do not truly care, as long as they get what they have been told and conditioned to believe that they need. However, the vast majority of what they receive is never spiritually supportive to them. Yet, they continue to accept and to allow themselves to be forced into accepting the negative social programming and processes when, to the truly spiritually conscious of the world, these processes and programming only serve to heighten and tighten the control of Super Ego and its operatives.

The only time humans are subject to these negative conditions and are unaware of them is when they have etched-God-out and rely merely on the conditioning of their own egos, which is an extension of the Super Ego. The true God of love and oneness is the only true foundation of human life. No man or system should be over or in control of nature or the human existence. The dome that we call freedom and this egotistical control system we relate to as civilization were devised by a few selfish men and women who thought they knew what was socially and spiritually right for everyone. In as much as the human who may complain about or openly enjoy the pleasures and freedoms civilization affords them, bar none, those nations that provide this structured and orderly democratic society is the best ego control system on Earth for the human being, subject to an egotistical world.

Why? Because we know of other societies that allow little or no freedom. I call this reality the acceptance of the lesser of two evils. Although we have not considered universal oneness, love or sharing for all of humanity. And sadly, only those who truly follow the direction of the Creator and of Creation are spiritually endowed to the extent that they know the difference and the difference is that all that is provided comes from the same ego control system whether lesser or more. It is all evil. Unfortunately, there are only a few of those individuals in the world today. How do we know this? Because most humans have been economically and politically forced to be selfish.

The selfish members of a society only care about individual survival or the survival of their own nuclear family or ethnic group. This is the diabolical attitude that has created many of the conditions we witness throughout the world on a daily basis.

Brothers and sisters around the world, the Creator of all heaven and earth has been good to us. It has given us all that we need and want. The gift of abundance is found in nature. It is our spiritual and human obligation to find a way to lift this dome of doom off us and free ourselves from the diabolical and egotistical energy that controls us. The negative social system under which we live controls and prevents us from returning to our loving creative oneness. We have no time to wait. We must begin our journey back yesterday! We are daily losing thousands of humans prematurely (genocide, murders, stress-related illnesses, starvation, etc). Vegetation is disappearing; we are losing the ozone layer and the rain forests. All of these conditions are due to the selfish of a few, greedy and controlling. We must make the turn and return to oneness. We must commit ourselves to returning to the direction of the Creator and the spiritual laws of creation. I know it will not be easy. The road back to oneness is very bumpy, strewn with the desires that we as individuals have fostered and cling to, the belief of being better than another so more deserving of that which is gifted to all of humanity, our person angst and our personal guilt. The deceptions we will confront on the road to oneness are legion. Yet, return we must, in humbleness, submit to love and allow ourselves to be endowed with the divine spirit of God, a spiritual loving vibration that is more powerful than any force man could ever understand.

As much as man would like to control life's destiny and all of creation, he cannot. He has certainly tried to do so, from the time of his submission to the Ego. Man's quest has been to conquer and to control the lives of his fellow man while controlling all that we depend on to sustain our survival on Earth. Well, for the most part, he has. There can still be a change, an individual change, and a change of values and of perceptions. There is that gifted mustard seed of faith in each one of us. All we need do is cultivate it. Then unite. The task of returning would not be nearly as difficult as we imagine. The spiritually loving individuals, those who have previously chosen to make the turn back to oneness are here to help. Love will overcome evil and can do so in short order, provided we simply unite against all social prejudices and silly childish social hang-ups and games.

A Loveless Society

In the human being, there is a need that must be cultivated, like any other life form in Creation. This process must start before and during the procreation period. Love is a force that vibrates unity and togetherness, want and need, a force that creates Oneness that is so powerful that it brings forth new life, in its support of all of life.

This force is promotable and received by the individual through the process of appreciation, appreciation for self and ones' creative environment. This wonderful and glorious need cannot be taught academically. It is instilled only through feeling, taught only by example, and examples are sorely missing in today's society.

The lack of love is the reason we have so much disrespect, confusion, destruction, and turmoil in our society, which makes this a very uncomfortable environment in which to be.

The reason nothing is being done about the disrespect evident in today's society is that we are taught to take advantage of the weak and the ignorant.

CARNAL - CARNAL - CARNAL - CARNAL - CARNAL - CARNAL

Total Image of Man

We are the total image of man. We have a very simply plan.
Just stand up, be a man. Be responsible. Be your own man.
Get yourself a strong family plan. Stop blaming the other man.
Because your woman is lonely.

Your woman is lonely. So…lonely.
She wants you to be her one and only.
Give her an image she can respect,
Not the horrors of abuse and neglect.

I hear children crying. Can't you hear them?
Children are crying because fatherly love is dying.
Give them an image they can respect.
We must start dealing with cause and effect.
You must be home to raise and correct.
Love does not come in a check.

Give them love, give them love. Lots and lots of love.
Singing about love and confusion
Because many are disillusioned.
Give them love, give them love.

We are the total image of man.
We are on a mission.
To recondition.

We are the total image of man. We have to take a stand.
To change this world because we can.
We are the total image of man,
And we have a simple plan.

All you gotta do is stand up and be a man.
Get yourself a family plan.
Be responsible.
Be your own man.

Carnal

The supreme egotistical understanding of the universe and all therein and none can have an understanding equal or greater than the Super Ego's.

This end-all-beat-all understanding allegedly possessed by the Super Egos can only come from an egotistical mind. The mind is the response and function of the brain, which is simply another part of the body. By the Ego's own definition, carnal means of the flesh and material world.

The mind records whatever it is programmed to record. We live in a loveless and an uber-selfish society so that is the information that the mind records.

The Greatest Punishment to the Human

The greatest punishment to a human is confinement. This tactic is used on every level of society: social segregation, economic segregation, religious segregation, prison (the hole) as segregation, educational segregation, communicational segregation, segregation in housing, segregation in employment, and the segregation of the human body throughout the civilized world.

Confinement is the cutting-off of one from the world in which he lives, for the sole purpose of controlling him, which only stimulates the demonic state known as desire. This desire is indeed demonic in that it castrates a man, leaving him without knowledge or the means by which to satisfy or to achieve his desires.

What kind of a mind would organize and structure a system that would deprive the human of knowing and appreciating his own mind and body and, instead, promote the fear of both? The human is afraid to explore his own body. For the most part, he is even ashamed of it. We have minds and bodies with natural spirit that functions the same way, but the promoters that control the system under which we live have us behaving as if we are all vastly different from one another in size, shape, color, and basic machination. This perception of difference intensifies the demonic fear of our own bodies. Because this intense behavior is extended to every level of human social life, the human body has become a self-destructive lethal weapon.

Fear of Self

The suppression of the natural spiritual order of God creates a negative energy called ego (etching-God-out). The constant cultivation of this practice promotes the development of a Doppelganger, which is an evil destructive energy used to destroy self and others.

The most entrenched program and indoctrination is fear of self. It is a subtle, gentle attack on ones innocence. This program and indoctrination are very effective because they are instituted at birth by our own parents.

Parents instill fear so well with us because they are unaware of what they are doing. Why? Because they are following the program that they were given.

The test? Touch yourself on a "private part" within a public space, whether your body dictates that you do so (as in the case of an unzipped fly or a wedge of underwear) or whenever you feel, albeit simply for a moment, that your body actually belongs to you to do with as you please.

Love is not a duty. Love is something we do when we are committed to the natural nature of true unconditional love. My family is a product of the ego. The natural unconditional human loving family is procreated from true unconditional love. It does not submit itself to the pronoun "my" or limit itself. It is extended, with only one responsibility: to heal those who have been deceived or who have fallen short.

True Carnal Knowledge

From the beginning of the human's introduction into the world, the infant child is force fed a host of lies. First, we learn to inflict and to appreciate pain. You know the smack on the butt, the swat that takes us from our bliss to life outside of ourselves. Then we encounter the indoctrination required to accept artificial light after living in natural darkness for nine months. Most children are not breast fed, so they accept milk from another animal, usually from a goat or a cow. If not from these two animals, the child gets a milk substitute comprised of a concoction of chemicals.

The intellectual reasons supporting the latter are: to some mothers with infants, breast-feeding does not come naturally, that the mother is just too lazy to breastfeed and for economical reasons, i.e. the mother must work and cannot remain at home to nurse. Many babies receive artificial sweetener and bleached sugar. The introduction of these artificial substances is increased and reinforced from the crib to the casket even though studies prove that there are definite, traceable effects that artificial substances, once ingested, have on human beings throughout our lifetimes.

When humans are just babies, innocent, blank and free, we know nothing of this world and its rules; laws, values, morals, etc. We walk around nude without shame or hang-ups. Just innocent and free. We know nothing about the labels or functions of our own body parts. As children, we are simply innocent and free. Everything that comes after this stage of innocence is ego-instructed.

We learn rights and wrongs, good and bad, and knowledge of all other things directly from our parental influences. The human is the only animal in captivity that continues to drink milk after weaning from its mother's breast and it is my belief that this continuation accounts for many physical and mental disorders.

In the natural unification order, it takes a village to raise a child, subject to the understanding and commitment of all of the adults to be role models and parents, which makes us all responsible for the problems of our human children as they grow into adulthood. They become social leaders, teachers, professors, scientist, conscience killers and out-right murders. Good, bad or indifferent, it is all of our doing. All for the sake of and in the nature of the ego.

Conquest to Control the Creator

Man immemorial has been on an extremely intense mission to control or to conquer the Creator. His intellectual egotistical mind has lead him to believe that he can sit down with God, talk and reason with him and let the true God know that there is another way Creation could have been achieved. Well, like all missions of the Super Ego, it has never absolutely finished.

Man has looked everywhere endlessly for the true Creator, but to no avail. Moreover, should he continue to search the dark and disjointed alley ways of his past meandering, man will never find the

Creator. Man has looked in clouds, in outer space, within the layers of the earth, in the seas and in the oceans, with no success. Why? The Super Ego will not allow man to find God.

In order for man to actually experience and to accept his true self, he must divorce himself from his selfish, materialistic mindset, which means that he must separate himself from his own ego so that the Super Ego can be destroyed. The Super Ego is committed to never allowing these actions to occur so it, the Super Ego, continues to treat the human race like children, manufacturing and promoting bigger and more colorful toys, and presenting these toys to humanity in the name of his gods---gods of commerce and commercialism, gods of investment and advertising, etc.

Super Egos lead humanity to believe that we will be or are being blessed when we are able to purchase their toys, whether they are computers, automobiles, household electronics, cellular telephones or music mediums. This "toys as reward" phenomenon is a well-executed example of organized chaos. By believing that we need or deserve the toys, for whatever reasons, we allow the Super Ego to reign and so it continues, selfishly and self-righteously manipulating humanity.

Man will never find the true God until he relinquishes his relationship with his ego. Man will never conquer or control Creation because he did not create it nor can he reproduce it. However, man can find the true God. The path of return is very simple. Man must accept his true spiritual and physical self, not as a master or a controller of creation, but as a mere part of creation, with love and appreciation for all that has been given.

Man's mission to find the true God has been a long, partially committed and arduous journey. It will continue to be so as long as man refuses to accept true, unconditional Love. For it is in true love that man finds his true self and in his true self-man discovers that God has always been with him.

In truth, the Creator is not above or below man. The Creator is a part of us all and all are part of It. The concept of an all-supreme God comes from the understanding that there is someone above all things. Well, this is merely an egotistical ploy created by Super Ego. The Super Ego wants all of humanity to support its assertion that it is the supreme power force, the supreme "know it all" and controller of all that is tangible and real within the limits of its own understanding. Yet, there has to be something greater and more powerful that is responsible for all that is not understood.

At different times and in different places, that which could not be understood by rulers has been explained in different ways: the Boogie Man, the Lady in White, fairies, the Loch Ness Monster, Big Foot, etc. However, none of these or any of their predecessors had lasting effect. Thus the necessity of creating an end-all-beat-all, a universal, all-seeing black hole of unlimited power, potential and awe (i.e. fear), an entity with the ability to strike men dead for failure to adhere to strict policies, whether the policies be in an individual's best interest or not.

Super Ego determined that it was necessary to create a god, of its own creation, complete with human emotions (jealousy and anger) and human frailties (limited patience). This god of ego creation has been in place for more than 2000 years and is "responsible" for countless atrocities against humanity and creation.

The creation of a human-like god supports the Super Ego's separatist process and program; separating humanity from the true Creator allows the Super Ego to control and to direct humanity according to its own agenda, utilizing tricks, schemes and punishment. The true understanding of a supreme Creator implies the knowledge that It is one presence; evident within all of humanity and creation, and that love is the energy that holds it all together.

The supreme order is the total unification of all that is, or is not, as nothing can be excluded. All is good, with love. The acceptance and understanding of this reality is where we find the almighty Creator, the supreme existence, the complete loving Oneness.

Over time, many writers have accepted and have referred to Jesus, to other religious representatives and to their words) as "the rock." This simply meant that these persons were directly sent by the

Creator, that they embodied the Creator or that they were the spiritually divine and anointed surrogates of the Creator.

These so-called representatives of the natural order of love had responsibilities, which included laying-out a solidified foundation for all human beings to follow, a blue print that would keep all of humanity and Creation within a loving balance, a supportive order.

Well, I am not as old as time, and I do not profess to be, but for the time I have been here, and the recorded times before my birth which I have studied, I am convinced that these conditions have not existed on Earth. To the contrary, my experiences and those recorded throughout the annals of time signify that just the opposite has been true.

Just think, for a moment, how the world would look if all of humanity subscribed to the notion that love was the only universally practiced political system. Justice would not be as we live it today, "just-us," currently coupled with the "I got mine, you get yours" ideas. We have too many people who have power yet practice the idea of "to hell with them," meaning all of the rest of us. Imagine a loving, universal, solid balance, where each man is measured by social and spiritual strength, in support of his brethren, with one slogan: "I am my brother's keeper."

What is most interesting is that well over half of the world is subject to three religions and all of these profess to be committed and subject to a loving Creator, a Creator who promotes unconditional love. There have been wars, since time began, complete with the killing of humanity and the destruction of Creation, most waged in the name of and supported by dominant religions.

It appears to me that the majority of religions use their holy books for social propaganda and for control. The Gods their followers submit to are the Gods of money and of guns, for the purpose of supreme power and control.

In a world with thousands of religions, one has to stop to ask why only three of them are known the world-over. There are only three religions promoted and always in the news. For those of you who may not be able to identify these three religions, they are, respectively, Christianity, Islam and Buddhism, which runs a distant third.

I hope that last kernel of truth has sparked your curiosity and it would be natural for you, reader, to think in the conventional way, to consider these three religions with respect, because most of us have been taught to revere God/Gods. However, look more closely because just the opposite is true.

We have not been taught to respect a God or Gods because of their reverential beneficence but because of their guns. Moreover, these three religions have the best and the biggest guns of all religions practiced in the world today. These dominant religions have the largest human destructive weapon arsenals in the world. Neither of these religions depends on the image of their Gods (that they project and promote worldwide) nor do they depend on their professed collective sect-sanctioned love for humanity to resolve their ills; they depend on guns.

These three dominant religions were founded on greed, on violence, on selfishness, and on the desire to control Creation, absolutely, by forcing all people to believe in their selfish doctrines in order to control and to direct humanity for their own benefit. How do I know this to be true? Because there have been countless instances, throughout recorded time, when members of these three religions have encountered individuals who were not yet associated with either religion and these folk, innocent of the religion, were told that they had a choice: either embrace the theology or die.

The authors of these three religious ideologies have given their followers and believers the right to believe that they are the chosen ones. Their understanding of the Creator and of Creation is absolute and ordained directly by God. These religions are so well constructed, organized and promoted that the followers are completely blind. They cannot see that only the hierarchy are benefitting materialistically from their material Gods.

You may ask why I refer to these Gods as materialistic. I do so because this is the only way these

Gods have been presented and represented; not in a spiritually loving fashion, suggesting that people work together, daily, to cultivate and to promote a loving, shared balance, striving to make the world a loving and pleasant place for all to live. Instead, these religions continue to force their respective ideologies, condemning and discrediting all who do not fall into line and accept their fodder, which ultimately causes friction, confusion, distrust, and hatred.

These intolerable conditions are always created by the religious leadership, which is never thinking about the interest of the masses. These negative conditions create atmospheres that have historically led to war and to countless other situations (read "skirmishes"). War is a state in which guns and other weapons of mass destruction are utilized. And "praise God and pass the ammunition," bespeaks a sad yet true reality that continues and that will continue as long as the masses are blind to or drunken by the false indoctrinations of ideologically materialistic Gods, Gods created by the selfish ego, created for the total control of all of humanity, Creation and the supreme celestial order.

Some may ask how false indoctrinations took root. This occurred, over time, whenever these dominant religions conquered and took control of all of nature's fruits and natural resources within a targeted region. The conquerors then ordained that only they had the right to disseminate said resources. From there, they gifted a small portion of resources to some, larger portions to others and nothing to most. All in the name of their conquering God.

Over time, these tactics convinced the local common folk within the target area to become religious adherents and to believe that all that had occurred was truly the will of the God bestowed upon them, thereafter known as a kind and loving God whom they submitted to in order to receive relief. This process works and it has worked the world-over for centuries.

Moreover, this system dictates that those who have been the most deprived believe that they have done something wrong (even if the offense was committed within their blood line generations prior to their birth), that they have not worked hard enough or that they have not prayed well enough in order to receive blessed relief from their deprivation. I refer to this phenomenon as "the pie in the sky syndrome." The leaders always taunt the followers with their riches and treasures, successfully convincing the latter that their stolen and innocent blood-soaked bounty is their rightful blessing from God.

The Origin of the Ego

Man must go back to the basic understanding of creation and surrender his egotistical, intellectual, materialistic mind to the Divine loving vibration of nature. Man can no longer depend on egotistical gods. These tricks and games are almost at an end because the lesser egos around the world are becoming more aware and exposed to the falsities they are being offered.

Ego is an acronym that means the etching out of God or, more simply, etching-God-out. God is the total unification and embodiment of Creation. By this point of the book, we should all be able to understand that, as described herein, that love has to be the creative spirit. Why? Because the opposite of love is hate and hate only breeds destruction.

Well, by this definition, the Ego is an erratic, confused, destructive ball of energy. Why not? There is no such thing as being able to etch-God-out. Everything relies on the power of the universe. However, along with Creation comes the power of choice and it is choice that allows the energy of desire. The desire to do all that is good and productive to benefit a loving oneness. Yet at some point in life, the negative energy we relate to and have labeled Ego decided it would no longer return to or be a part of the original order of creation. It had its own agenda, ala Creation could be done another way: bigger, better, faster, and more beautifully. We must strive to rid of minds of this Ego-inspired insanity because, from their origins, everything was placed within Creation perfectly. Therefore, it is each man's responsibility to respect and to appreciate Creation.

From its inception, the Ego had all of the original powers and abilities granted to every aspect of Creation, but the Ego was not satisfied. Though it could travel the universe at will and transform itself from spiritual into physical and back again at will, somehow, at sometime and for some reason, the Ego became obsessed with the flesh. These are the very same conditions we deal with today, when children and adults alike are subject to and worshippers of flesh. They will do anything to beautify, to protect and to enhance their flesh, without even realizing that it is not them, failing to understand that they are being controlled and directed by the Ego.

The emphasis and praise given to the human body is insane. This insanity runs the gamut from sex to religion. The human must look a certain way; humans are killing themselves with exercise, operations and diets. Today's masses care little or nothing for the spirit. Most know little or nothing of the love of the true Creator.

The spiritual entity that the Creator created is gone, lost in the Ego. Yet the spirit of love has never left the Ego or humanity. It is always there, waiting patiently for man to surrender and to return to love. The true God is complete and unconditional love. It never gives up and it never gives out.

These feelings and vibrations that I have received from a life's experience and relations with nature and the universe, were not only meant for me. These feelings and vibrations were meant for me to share with all of humanity. This is what motivates me to write.

How do we get back? First, we must identify what is God's and what belongs to the Ego. Then we can determine how much control he Ego has over us. We know that all that is natural is a gift from God: the sun, moon, air, water, and all of nature. These things ask humanity for nothing. However, all of the things provided by the Ego arrive with a contingency---you must give something back, including your soul, and if you do not give back (mark for mark and measure for measure), the Ego condemns you to its hell for eternity.

If the Ego controlled the sun, it would charge humanity for sunlight and the same with the moon. The Ego would only provide night light for the ones it liked. If the Ego controlled all of the water, all of the air and all of the sand and rocks comprising the Earth, it would charge humanity as well. This sounds like the very same thing man is doing today. Now perhaps you can see that to identify what God gives verses what the Ego gives is not very difficult. All one has to do is to simply think outside of the box, your Ego.

If there were no Egos, there would be no Super Ego. The Super Ego is comprised of the Egos that are more committed to proving to God that their way is the better way and that the Creator's way is wrong. The more the Ego is committed to following this self-destructive path and adhering to the misdirection thereof, the more that individual Ego is empowered with tricks and weapons to use to defeat those Ego that are less committed yet that trod the same crooked path. The Super Egos, those who devised the crooked path, are absolutely committed to competition and games.

The games start with sex and with procreation, men and women competing to do or to control one or the other sexually. Then, procreation, whether involving a human baby or any other animal: the Ego commits itself to making a bigger, better, faster, stronger, smarter, and more beautiful offspring.

Most of the Ego's competition and games are with and about the flesh, never with the spirit of love and the true Creator. The Ego knows it cannot win in a competition against the Creator. The Ego's physical competition stops when it competes with brain against brain, religion, athletics on any level, and even its Egotistical self. Games and competition are the only way the Ego can last and sustain itself. The victor of its competitions is always rewarded by the Super Egos and other artificial gods.

The Ego does not make sacrifices unless it is assured of getting something in return. It must always receive praise and exaltation because it cannot stand on its own. This is the reason why the Ego always looks for someone to lean on or to use.

The Ego is a masterful game player. It even plays games with our social time. All of my life I have heard one group of friends saying "I will be glad when things change" while another group of friends might say, "I hope things never change." I, at one point in my life, found these opposing viewpoints confusing. After all, both groups represent people within the same society who were all subject to the same prejudices.

Well, I'm older and wiser and now know that the comments of the two groups represent an old Egotistical game: denying and depriving one group while making promising and seeming concessions to another group, which leaves the two groups in opposition to one another---the supposedly privileged ones taunt and tempt the lesser one with the luxuries they have been afforded.

A few of the people within this society who have less, materialistically speaking, always seem to be bored, but not the on-looker who has true spiritual understanding. Why not? It is spiritual understanding that allows the onlooker to know that those who have less to commit themselves to (from a materialistic stance) appear to be bored because, in fact, they are. They are bored of Egotistical games.

The Ego has every facet of society, from church to the white house, supporting its Egotistical games. The Super Egos, which are consumed by competition, control and confusion, will never change the games it plays because the games work.

The lesser Egos, over time, begin believing that there is something wrong with them or that God has denied them and they grow frustrated. This game has nothing to do with the true loving God. It is all Ego.

Creation has given us all the same seasons, the sun, the moon, the stars, air, and water from the time we arrived here on Earth. For the most part, every human is satisfied with these things. These gifts are not boring and we have not grown tired of them. The reason I know that humans have not grown tired of the gifts provided us by the true Creator is that most of us want to continue living. Therefore, you see there are not many people who are actually bored with living; they are simply bored with playing the game wherein the deck is stacked against them.

Moreover, for all the human beings who seem trapped inside the boxes of anger, frustration and fear, you too can win. You must, however, identify and acknowledge that you are infected. You are simply a carrier of an Ego germ. Drop your Ego and stand. Then you can get out of the box.

Man must go back to the basic understanding of creation and surrender his Egotistical, intellectual, materialistic mind to the divine loving vibration of nature. Man no longer can depend on Egotistical Gods. The tricks and games are almost at their end.

The lesser Egos around are becoming more aware and more exposed. They are tired of empty dreams and promises, lies, physical and mental abuses and death. They want change! Not the kind of change that is prompted by the appointment or the election of a president, preacher or king. All of these titles represent the Egotistical system and the results of their changes is always the same. There is victory for a select few with despair and disappointment for the masses. The only hope for all the lesser Egos of the world to save themselves from this diabolical social movement is to surrender their Egos to true love. Come together and start the promotion of an international campaign for One Love for all. There is no other way. If we, the lesser human Egos, continue to depend on the Super Ego to change our human condition, we deserve what we get.

Men of the Super Ego have always promised change for the masses but with no true intention. You cannot change or solve a problem with a problem; you can only create more problems and bigger problems. This pattern has been established by the Super Ego. This pattern continues and will continue until we, the lesser Egos, surrender to true love.

Yes, we have been screwed from the time of conception to the understanding and submission to our materialistic God. You know that one that favored one group of people over others. They give rewards in exchange for the taking of your selfhood: plenty of materialistic toys for you to play with.

Yes, state of relying only on intellect is where you lost your connection with the true loving spirit of the Creator. We started rationalizing the free loving will of Oneness and the Creator. In our rationalizations, if we did not have the most of a thing, having less of it than another person was not to be accepted. Intellect, devised by the selfish Super Ego, is not going to accept anything else except selfishness. Selfishness promotes selfishness to all levels of society, and as long as it works in our behalf it does not matter, i.e. "I got mine, now get yours," even after all has been taken and nothing is left. This attitude permeates our society today and that we are content with until we ourselves are without. It is then that we want the whole world to stop and to respond to our needs. Yet the band plays on.

This is a system of organized chaos. It will only allow you to survive within set limits, committed to never allowing you to live freely or to achieve your full spiritual potential. Any human who feels that they are living free and who feel that they have reached their full potential will never acknowledge the limitations imposed by this society because they are blinded by their own individual Egotistical and material success. For the most part, they are satisfied with society just as it is.

Energy and Power

The power of God is love, unconditionally. Man has a spiritual obligation to appreciate and to respect his own existence, i.e. to be responsible to and for the human procreative process. Moreover, man has a spiritual obligation to execute and to promote his right to make the choices necessary in order to maintain a harmonious earthly atmosphere of peace, unity, love, respect, and economic balance. Said spiritual obligations, if freely exercised, promote in man the need to allow nothing to deny him the right of his own autonomy.

The only forces that prevent man from fulfilling his obligations to appreciate and to respect self are greed and control. These forces, employing their tools of money and guns, prevent the harmony. First, the guns are introduced. They are used to force you into submission and fear. Then comes the economic deprivation, which creates desire and control. These actions are not of the Creator, but of selfish, egotistical, power-hungry human beings who desire to be gods.

Over time, many men from different tribes, ethnic group and nationalities have tried to execute these rights, even after guns and economic deprivation are used against them. This is the point when, after the leading agitator has been disposed of, when ego employs religion and forces it on the masses. A religion subject, of course, to a God imbued with the characteristics and the agenda of the gun-toting conqueror.

Sickness

All sickness is the same, no matter whether it is mild or severe. If you cannot identify or accept your sickness then you can never begin to heal.

The most dangerous human social disease is egotism. It is a sickness passed down from generation to generation, human to human. The sole purpose and mission of this pandemic is social control and deception, which ultimately leads to distrust, disengagement, separation and discomfort, all of which are components of the ego.

Once infected by this disease, you are then committed to selfishness and survival is the greatest necessity to human social existence. This makes Ego extremely difficult to identify without the intervention of love. The Ego hates and avoids love because it is well aware that any acceptance of love cancels it out.

Religion

Religion is the school that most people attend in search of their false spiritual selves. Denominations are the subjects in which false knowledge is obtained.

Churches

I always thought that church was a building erected to house the spirit of the true God. Now I know, as does any spiritually sound human being (one who is in contact with his spiritual self), that the Creator cannot be housed, harnessed, or controlled. Yet, the conventional church continues to instigate this fallacy. The spirit of the Creator is everywhere, available to all who submit. With that thought, I began to ponder the nature of the God housed within our churches. Could it be a God contrived from man's own selfish ego? Especially in view of this fact: there are thousands of churches and most seem to me to have their own special Gods. These Gods serve only to benefit the specific congregations who serve them. The members who are from a line of big money, power or intellect, reap the most benefits from their God. The congregants without the proper credentials get less and, oftentimes, nothing at all.

I have often asked why, in a world where we have more churches and religions than houses of pleasure and ill repute, why the societies of this world are not getting any better. Why has man failed to learn how to love and to share his God-given Earth with all of humanity? It seems to me that man is getting further and further away from the ideas of Oneness and love for his universal brother.

Reportedly, themes of love and unity are the basis of all churches and religions. Truth is not necessary when all men and women around the world are living in accord with the vibrations of these themes. Yet today's world is in dire need of love, unity and truth. The Spirit of Love should be center-stage, shown and lived-out daily. We were taught that churches are the houses of God. Their focuses should be, then, love and unity. However, today's churches focus, too much, on everything except true, unconditional love.

Churches teach that there is only one God and only one love. Why then do we have so many churches and religions? This is clearly a contradiction. Most churches are in spiritual turmoil. They cannot distinguish between the love of the true spiritual Creator and that of the material world. Money, fashion and power seem to be their focus.

Yet, there was a time when churches were centers for people to gather and to solve social problems. Today's churches are not even doing that. Previously, people from the same cities, towns and countries would not come together because of social status, color, race, nationality, or religion. Yet, church leaders were preaching 1God, one love and 1church, subject to the 1God. Today the conditions have changed somewhat, but they still have a long way to go.

Many men have called churches "the synagogues of Satan" and have called religion "the opiate of the masses," i.e. a place to house the people of a given society in order to keep them high, confused and misdirected, which better enables the Super Egos to take advantage of and to maintain control over them.

I have waited a long time for the churches' attitudes to change, but it seems to me that their attitudes are getting worse. The conditions in the churches do not seem to be leading the congregations away from a materialistic world and into a spiritual state of peace, love and spiritual tranquility. As much as churches help a few people to understand, confront and overcome their individual social problems, these churches are light years away from demonstrating what they profess to stand for.

If the church leaders today contain a fiber of spirituality, then they must know by now that they are following the wrong Gods, teaching, preaching and misleading their congregations with false information.

I have always had a problem with the Holy books from which church leaders preach. Most of these leaders promote the idea that said books contain the divine word of the true Creator. This has always been a difficult idea for me to accept. Why? Because if I am to accept that their books are holy and divine, then I must also accept that the dictionary is holy and divine. After all, the dictionary is the book from which we, the readers, get our definitions and our pronunciations.

From the perspective of the readers, without a dictionary and the knowledge of how to use it, the holiest of religious text is just a bunch of words that mean nothing. Moreover, history reveals that the men who were responsible for the creation of the dictionaries were not men committed or subject to the true spirit of universal Love and Oneness. Quite the opposite is true: they had BIG Egos, which means that the holy books are founded on the nature and energy of the Ego, which is selfish, which intentionally misleads and which confuses for its own selfish gain.

Nature and Creation cannot speak in words; they only speak in and with sound, feeling and vibration. Man gives these feelings and vibrations words. These words can be useful, depending on one's mindset and intent. When a human, founded in spirituality, looks for true love and direction from the true Creator, they get a feeling of goodwill, togetherness and love. If man's mindset is Ego-founded, they get a selfish, boastful, exclusive, and proud feeling. Everything supported by the Ego is always right for you, bigger and better, and the Ego always knows what is good for all of humanity, even when it knows nothing of the problem and has less true concern about what caused the problem.

Religion is a diversion from the true Creator of Love. This is only one aspect of the Creator, too. You see, the Creator's divine Spiritual Love is also unconditional. There is no room for disorder or division. In fact, anything that does not love repels, like water from a duck's back.

Because the order of divine Spiritual Love is love-spawned, it can support only all that is in a loving unconditional fashion. It is the only true and solidified order. Which means all that is came from Love. Nevertheless, at the same time, it does not mean that separation or divorcing oneself from Love is not allowed. It is a choice, meaning that you are on your own to select which act you will take. On your own to create or to invent whatever substitution you wish. Love is always there to support your choice. However, the consequences are all yours.

Consequence is the result of an action and the action was to separate from the divine solidified order of love. Hence, religious wars began, confusion among the masses followed and many Gods were mis-created.

Churches today care little or nothing to help or to solve social problems and the society and its leaders are where most of the congregations' problems come from. Our churches have signed an

42

agreement of separation of church and state. Worse still, churches are tax-exempt; therefore, the hands of today's church leaders are, in truth, bound tightly.

Organized Religion

Organized religion is a system of control instituted to offer a person social direction. Its goal is absolute control.

Religion is a drug that impairs the mind and it can take form in reality, creating whatever fantasy or distraction wished for, inviting intense fear, false happiness and obscene pleasure.

Using religion allows a person (ego) to create their own Gods in order to serve and to satisfy one's own needs. Most humans only need a God when they are afraid or are in trouble, physically or socially. The image and nature of a God is usually based on location, ethnicity, language, and perceived need. This is one of many e-Gods.

These ego-Gods are similar to the physicians within our society in that each party is committed to doing just enough in order to keep you coming back to them, never allowing a person to become self-dependent.

E-Gods know that all that is natural loves, is spiritual-grounded and is free but, because e-Gods oppose the nature creative order, they only give to a few, sometimes, and always for a price. An imitation of life is what you get, after toiling in every way to achieve the specified benchmarks erected by an e-God: artificial, material, synthetic, and generic.

The Ego

It has been said that the Devil is the Super Egos of the true Creator, but anyone who has a bit of spiritual presence knows better. They are aware that the true Creator is all of everything that is good, and that all means nothing of value in this Egotistical world. There is no need for the Ego or for the Super Egos.

The understanding of the Creator and Ego leads me to believe that when the Creator recognized evil in its midst that evil was cast out. However, Love cannot cast out that which is a part of itself no more than a loving mother can cast-out one of her children. Even if the child leaves her, the mother's love goes with the child.

Love promotes choice and choice is where the Ego chooses to separate and where it is committed to separating everything within its path. It even separates Egos---the lesser Ego is separated from the Super Egos. The method used by the Ego to separate is something from nothing.

The Ego gives value and titles to nothing so that it be perceived as something, at least in the mind's eye of the human being. A classic example of the "something from nothing" method is evident when considering the pet rock fad of post-WWII America, or any other phenomenon that once captured the collective attention of this society, spawning an onslaught of consumerism: the Cabbage Patch Kids, Hula Hoops, the Rubik's Cube, patent-leather tennis shoes, poodle skirts, the 1965 Corvette, cellular telephone, cable television, Manolo Blatnik shoes, etc. The Ego's purpose is to place all kinds of things (toys) on every path that a human being could travel.

The Ego's attacks can be overt or covert, but they are always mildly perceptible, at first. Initially, the Ego approaches in the form of agreement or of satisfaction of another's selfishness. Said acts create, support and promote false love. This is the love that we can see throughout this society, i.e. "I must give you something of value to please you and I must openly agree with you in order for me to demonstrate the power of my love for you," even if the subject the Ego approached is wrong, known or shown to commit atrocities against other humans or even against self. Again, this selfishness bespeaks the quality of love that is prevalent in the world today, supported by religious, political and social strata.

These religious, political and social strata in support of this latter-day rendition of love are supported by the energies of fear and selfishness. Fear is evident in the Ego's need to conquer while selfishness is evident in Ego's need to control. The Ego wants total control over self and over all of Creation, forcing and demanding that everything in its path submit to its direction or perish. Many humans have and are perishing today because these Egotistical systems are in place and are fully functioning.

Egotistical systems, world-wide, are supported by human beings feigning allegiance to their Gods and governments, Gods and governments that, by the way, respond to you at times, or sometimes, depending on the completeness of one's submission, devotion or response to the superbly Egotistical process.

The Ego has its own beginning for human life. A life, a place, a race and even a complexion for the first human being, but not for the other animals in Creation, which only leads me to believe that everything was placed here, as per the dictations of the true Creator, in preparation for the arrival of the human. Logically then, Ego's God placed everything here for its own selfish ends and to promote self-glorification, especially from the lastly created human. Therefore, this Ego-God responds to its most dutiful servant, the Ego, based obviously, upon the strength of their personal relationship. Right?

The true Creator, however, is a part of everything and everything is a part of it. Therefore, there is no need for a personal relationship. All is one and one is all within the natural order of Creation. True love never leaves anything. It is always there, waiting for the energy to surrender. The Ego will only surrender when love becomes an epidemic and infects every living thing that Ego has subtly seduced away from Oneness.

When the time arrives wherein love becomes epidemic, Ego will be left with nothing. Ego fears this nothing. The Ego can only survive with things, things that it has created for the purpose of control. The Ego cannot survive in the absence of its toys. The Ego will have to choose, either to submit to love or to destroy itself.

Why don't we cut the bullshit! We should know by now that the universal unification of Oneness or unity can never be achieved unless we accept one simple fact: this is a war of Egos.

Dominate Super Egos are trying to remain in control of everything while suffering lesser Egos are deeply entrenched in their struggle to rule. It is sad that these lesser Egos cannot identify that they are being influenced, to their own destruction. This Ego-infection is devastating every civilized society on Earth, causing all manner of disease, separation and death. Total chaos completely supported by reason, purpose, excuses, and fully justified by the ignobly "righteous" Ego-God.

The Alter Ego

The ego does not discriminate. It shares itself with everything that separated from the true spiritual Oneness. The purpose of this equality is to make certain that its campaign to separate and to control never ends.

The energy of the alter-ago was mis-created during the initial separation and it has been passed down to those few who are worthy. You must be totally committed to something in order to receive it. The others, those desiring to be a part of the egotistical game, do not understand what a mess of it they make nor can they understand, as they are blinded by their desire to be included.

How do we know that the Ego cannot go forward and that its forward is backwards? If we, the ones who have begun to surrender our egos to the energy of spiritual oneness, can recognize these things if we would but stop for a moment and think. Consider man's innermost desire is to recreate self and to conquer life. These two things sustain his existence. He is here already and he already exists yet he cannot accept this and simple live a loving life. Man's ego prevents him from accepting his reality.

Man's ego separated from love and nothingness by choice. Choice is the reason it goes backward. It is simply re- accepting what it chose at the onset of the separation (not to remain part of), which renders the ego only capable of reflecting on its past and on every pleasure it remembers. Ego re-creates every pleasure it experienced in order to control its existence, in order to make itself important by making experiences into something.

The lesser only understands everything to be something. Therefore, it plays with the toys that the alter ego has created, invented or made. The alter ego believes these toys to be real. However, all that is spiritually created lasts forever. The ego's toys last, well, you know. Just think about it.

I remember a time when I first recognized my ego and how vigilant it was in me. My recognition occurred while I lived with my third wife. I thought I had control of myself, without realizing that my ego was truly in control of me. Not realizing until I had lost control. That is when I recognized that I, too, was controlled and I realized what the word freedom meant: free as long as you are doing what I want you to do.

Just consider being committed to a process for most of your life that you are not even aware exists, then realizing that the time has arrived for self-exorcism. If you have ever tried to free yourself from egotistical programming, you understand what I mean. The mere idea of freeing oneself from such a program is frightening, and actually beginning the freeing process is one of the most difficult things in the world.

The Lesser of Two Evils

The lesser of two evils is still evil and slavery is a product of the Ego. Poverty, self-denial and deprivation are all products of your Ego.

Evil is denying one the right to find the path back to nothingness. In order to achieve nothingness, one must first recognize their own Ego in order to avoid being controlled and / or influenced by other Egos.

The greater Ego has knowledge and the support of other great Egos. This multi-tentacle approach is inevitably passed-down from one generation to the next. No one knows where it comes from.

The Ego has no life, yet everything that the Ego deals with does, even and including the smallest cell. Yes, the Ego has no origin for life has no beginning and no ending. The Ego creates and it promotes its own stories and it calls them Creationism and Religion. I know that Life comes from nothing, because the state of nothingness is not known by the Ego.

Why does man pay a price for all the things that come from the natural order of Nature if a loving God provided all things on Earth? Why are you compelled to pay a price for anything that you need? The reason that you must pay for "clean air", "clean water", etc., is that you have not been taught to worship a truly loving God. Instead, you worship a God of value, thus you must pay for the life and for the death the God of value exacts.

Can we worship or respond to the true God? Yes! Devalue all that you value! You can have possessions and not value them. The sparrow does. So can you. Keep your eyes on the sparrow. The sparrow builds his nest and leaves it, to be used by other birds. No Egos control the sparrow, so it can build a nest, dwell therein, and then leave it to be inhabited by others. The sparrow does not value the nest as one of its possessions after the purpose for which it was built has been served.

The Ego places value on everything. If you doubt the validity of my last assertion, then complete the following exercise:

> Stand or sit anywhere you choose. Meditate
> and concentrate on nothing for 20-minutes.
> Everything around you will become nothing.

Love-hate relationships cannot exist. Where there is true spiritual love, there hate cannot enter. Like water off a duck's back, love repels hate.

The greater Ego (evil) has an intense need to control. It is consumed by fear. It does everything to pass this confused corrupted energy down, from generation to generation, for the sake of absolute control---by whatever means necessary. Consider the genocides recorded within the past millennium.

The lesser Ego submits and accepts the greater Ego because it has not been given the right of self-choice (free choice). The lesser chooses its direction from the greater Ego.

The greater Ego, having absolute control, creates a system of misinformation, misdirection and confusion to prevent the lesser Ego from recognizing the power of true self, i.e., the power to create one's own heaven and hell.

Heaven and hell are concepts, systems of co-dependence that greater Egos used to nullify a lesser Ego's ability to rely on the power of self, rendering the lesser forever crippled by the greater Egos.

Guns, God and Education

For 500 hundred years or more, humans have been forced to believe, to do or to function, subject to the man or to the men who had the biggest gun. In previous times, he had used other instruments of control.

The controlling process never allowed the naïve and curious human minds to learn. Especially not in context with the conventional definition that educators give us. Quite the contrary, we are trained. Trained, just like any other animal.

Education, to the minds of most conventional students, is a system that affords them the ability to see and to serve the entire spectrum of life. Even more frightening, they believe that education gives them the right to look down their noses upon (to castigate and to separate themselves from) all those not as thoroughly exposed to the hallowed halls of education.

It is sad. If these students only understood that they are trained, similarly to any other tamed animal, say a pig then, perhaps, they too could see that, like a pig, they themselves are unable to think outside of the slop.

The Ego and Intellect

In my life, I have found many things interesting, but none more interesting than words. The mystery of words, like how did they get their meanings, how did man develop letters to formulate words and who chose certain letters to form certain words? How did humans match words with human feeling and emotions? Were the etymologists committed to the loving creation of Oneness?

These are just some of the mysteries I find when considering words. Yet, I find words both exciting and intriguing. However, I have never found a word that could define the depth and innermost feeling of true spiritual love.

Neither have I found the love I feel is necessary in order to fill that emptiness that dwells inside of me, that feeling of complete Oneness and true protection, a love powerful enough to ward off anything that is non-loving, a love that cannot be affected by the negative overtures of this maniacally egotistically society. A love infected only by love, unconditionally, with social desires free from materialistic wants. A love that is one into one, between creation and me. A love that looks only to itself for its needs and wants. In all that I have experienced, never have I found a word or a phrase that would capture that spiritual vibration.

There was a time when a man's word was his bond. At that time words and phrases had little loving spiritual substance. Today's verbal communication, by contrast, is devoid of any spiritual loving substance. Words are completely empty. Words mean nothing, especially when we reference love, equality, justice, and Oneness, though these are the very things man claims he is and has been striving to achieve for the last 2-thousand years. It seems to me that with each social revolution, man gets further and further away from his alleged goal.

Man's ego will not allow him to accomplish the mission of equality because man refuses to surrender his ego to the loving Oneness. His ego allows him to control and to dominate other men, then to justify his actions in his materialistic God. A God that some men claim created his love-less words, words that men use to entertain and to impress, words that do so much more to promote disappointment, distrust, confusion, and death than they do to promote love. Words, I was taught as a child, God created. I was also told that God named all animals, a lie that lingers in the subliminal mind for all of one's life. These types of lies rape the individual of the required and God-given self-ambition needed in order to seek and to find a true understanding.

Yet, as much as the ego twisted and slants its words, they still intrigue me. I find that if you make true spiritual application to life, and use these ego-driven words well, the spirit of Love will manifest itself and will direct you to the true, creative, spiritual definition and understanding of words. The ego frowns on true spiritual understanding because this differs from its own biased and controlled understanding.

Words like "yes" and "no" can be destructive, especially when you are being questioned by an ego-driven mind. Many innocent men and women have been prosecuted and executed because they did not know to whom they were answering "yes" and "no."

The egotistical inquisitor would not allow the victim to explain the true spiritual understanding of what had occurred. The questioner was full of intellect. Thousands are dead and many more imprisoned because of this ego-driven process questioning.

Intellect destroys innocence and takes one away from the supreme spiritual understanding that all is one. The less one desires to come apart of a system, the more spiritual he is. The mission of the human ego is to conquer the mind and body of all things in Creation, and then to claim all for its own. If allowed, the human ego would ultimately suppress or wholly destroy the natural spirit of life via intellect, science or religion.

The Creator is the unification of all things and all things are nothing in It. There is no natural value system, only the one created by ego, for only ego needs labels and titles.

Selfish

Selfish is having an abundance of anything and not sharing where there is a need.

Selfish is legally taking the right to be from anyone for one's own selfish needs and control.

Selfish is the act of desiring harm to anyone for one's own gain.

Selfish is expressed through manipulating or taking something from anyone when you know that the thing taken is not your own.

Selfish is the support of any system that supports one group of people or nationality without the consideration for others.

Selfish is to think that you are responsible for self, when you do not know your own beginning.

Selfish is to think that God (the Creator) rewards individuals. You reward yourself by utilizing all that the Creator has given you.

Selfish is to promote fear without teaching that there is nothing to fear.

Selfish describes the act of depriving and inflicting pain simply because someone does not subscribe to or submit to an egotistical system of oppression.

All Having Nothing

All having nothing is one. All having all of everything is nothing. One. This explains the reasons why the Ego cannot accept true equality. The ego must keep the human in a state of desire---always wanting something or wanting more of something.

All for one and one for all is a rally cry for love. The ego will cease to exist in our everyday lives once this rally becomes a concerted international campaign. Instead, the Ego keeps humanity confused and divided.

The Ego Has No Place

The Ego has no place, for love destroys the Ego. Love blossoms from sacrifice. The Ego lives on trickery and on manipulation. Fear is the energy that carries and promotes the Ego. The Ego fears having to submit to anything outside of itself and Ego will do anything, bar no action, to exist.

Does love recognize the Ego? No, but Ego recognizes love. Ego's greatest fear is true love. Ego avoids direct contact with love, but it is always waiting, lurking obscurely, for a break, usually at a point of weakness, to attack you, or to attack the closest thing to you. Ego is excellent at attacking things that are innocent because the innocent are not aware of its existence.

The Definition of F-U-C-K

A definition for the word "fuck" is entering into any one place or space in order to commit evil. To aggravate, conquer or take over for one's own pleasure or desire. Once any of the preceding had occurred, "You've been fucked!"

The only reason anyone should enter anyone's space or place should be to bring or to share love.

"Fornication Under Carnal Knowledge" is the false information that is given our teachers and leaders. These falsehoods give us humans the right to justify fucking one another, i.e. if someone is weaker or has less knowledge than I have, I then have the right to take advantage of them. This thought process is taught and is practiced on every level of this society.

Trying to bring together a universal oneness in loving unity is an everyday, never-ending, thankless job. Use of brute force will not help to accomplish this endeavor. It can only be accomplished with love. There is no other way.

I will now provide an example from my personal life, an episode that, upon repeated reflection, helped me to understand how deeply steeped in my own ego, coupled with the satisfaction that I, too, epitomized the brute force "fuck you" energy. It is an episode that returned to my mind, repeatedly, and which helped to cultivated in me the need to write this book: late one Friday night, at approximately 1:00AM, the streets of Saigon, Vietnam were congested with people. Most were children. A kid, perhaps aged seven or eight, approached two of my friends and I and asked us for ten "p", which was a very small amount of money. We pushed the child away and laughed. He immediately responded and said, in fluent English, "Fuck you, motherfucker!"

From that night until this day, that child's response has haunted me. I could very well have given him the money he had requested but chose not to, only because I had been trained as a soldier not to give money to the citizens of the country I was helping to invade. Not even when I knew that the children I saw daily were, in fact, very hungry and, oftentimes, starving. These children were only trying to survive in a mess that they had not created. A situation we all find ourselves in every day.

How Can

How can stealing millions of dollars be more scandalous or more diabolical than killing millions of innocent men, women and children to satisfy an egotistical controlling process?

On Achieving Success in a Material World

In the material world, there is only one way to be successful and that is to think big and to commit self to die trying to get it. Success, that is.

Moreover, failing to make this commitment, you will live your life wondering, being envious, lying, and hating. The humans who have made this commitment are our heroes. They are the ones we want to emulate, by whatever means necessary. Therefore, we have accepted them as our heroes. Naturally, then, we kill self, our families, our neighborhoods, and our countries trying to achieving worldly success.

Resurrection, in a Sense

The Death of the Ego marks the resurrection of love. The energy of the Ego influences the reproductive process in human beings.

Should a mature, responsible man be forced, by social mores, rules and principles, to be interested in, to date or to marry a woman who has been abused and damaged due to the lack of appreciation she has received during her early life?

This question is most pertinent if you consider that it is not the mature and responsible man who damages the young woman. In truth, the damage is committed by a boy raised within the same society.

A boy, with scant experience negotiating through life, one lacking responsibility for himself and even the faintest understanding of how to be responsible for another, is given the right to date and to marry (though this second step rarely occurs) an as yet un-jaded young woman. Within this scenario, the young man lacks the life experience required to appreciate her beyond the realm of her flesh. Therefore, the boy woos the young woman, impregnates her, disappoints her, and then leaves her with a baby to raise all alone, to boot. How much damage must occur before our society changes its acceptance of child coupling with child and producing another child?

This society is doomed to continue producing generations of damaged and untrusting middle-aged women until it can see itself clear to only allowing mature and responsible men to take on the responsibility of the marrying, of loving and of guiding the young women. Considering, then, that it is the energy of Ego that clearly infects the American reproductive process, how can this society but produce offspring who ultimately, and oft times swiftly, fall prey to the same Ego energy as did their parents, and who commit the same actions?

Sex

Before a young man mounts a horse, he must or should have some knowledge of the responsibility of riding horses. Some have the ability to ride bare back while others need a saddle. Never the less, the rider knows the responsibilities that accompany the experience.

What we know as sexual intercourse is a natural, biological function. Just imagine if you had been taught that urinating and defecation were taboo, and those functions had been assigned all of the mystic and mystery associated with sex. Now imagine that you have to wait until you found someone empowered to sanction these other biological function before you could complete these acts. Try to envision the devastation possible to the biological and mental functioning of the human body if this were the case.

We are taught that sex is bad, then we experience it and it feels good, but it is still wrong, all of which spawns abstinence and or masturbation.

A male and female, having sex for the first time, is like a surgeon going to a body for the first time. We would hope that the surgeon has experience because, if he does not, he could make a mistake that could prove fatal or that may damage an individual (in this case, the female) for the rest of their life.

The responsibility of taking on child and family is not materialistic, not physical and not egotistical.

Romance - Man to Woman

Romance is the fantasy of wanting true unconditional love. In today's society, it only lasts for a short time. Why? Because romance occurs when you know you have a woman or a man to love. Whether it appears to the world to be a woman or a man does not matter. It is whatever the individual believes it to be. That is all that matters. The perception that the other person has everything you need and everything you want, for that moment in time. Moreover, you do not want that moment to ever end. You will give your life to sustain that moment.

Romance is when nothing means anything but the immediate relationship and you are in love with everything. That is when you realize that there is nothing more powerful than love. It is the spirit of love that has allowed that moment to exist, the moment when you feel and connect with all of Creation.

Complete joy.

For a moment.

Homosexual and Heterosexual Relationships

After years of surveying both men and women, in both the hetero and homosexual communities, I began to ask all whether they would bond with, create a union with or marry a partner who did not have the sexual organs with which they had been born. The response to my question, at least 95% of the time, was "No."

Unfortunately, there is little difference in the motives of today's citizens, those entering same-sex domestic partnerships. The majority of participants actively engaged in these unions, at least those I have encountered and questioned, indicate that their unions are based on the wrong things: egotistical lust and control. Void of true love. Unfortunately, these responses painfully resemble those I receive when I question members of traditional marriage.

KNOWLEDGE - KNOWLEDGE - KNOWLEDGE - KNOWLEDGE

Let Me Be Like a Tree

When it comes to my God
Let me be like a tree
Giving love and life to everyone
Unconditionally
Glorifying God by working
And being responsible for
All Creation daily, for all
The world to see
So let us see – Just a
Few things that come from
The never complaining tree
The air you breathe, so you can
Live at ease – the paper that
Makes the money you spend and
Never forget the rubber
That absorbs the bumps of
Car tires when
You ride these bumpy roads
A house for shelter and protection
From all types of weather
Never asking for anything – just giving unconditional Love
So when it comes to my God
Let me be like a tree
When the world seems against you
And they're treating you like mud
Find the nearest forest and give
A tree a hug – I guarantee you'll find
Unconditional love.

What is the Creator?

The Creator is the total summation of all things living and dead. The Creator is the unification of all things conceivable and not yet conceived. This endless unification process has formed a vibration so powerful it can do whatever it wills whenever it wills it.

The human mind cannot conceive or imagine the full and complete capacity of the Creator. The mind breaks the concept down and separates it into portions, creating many Gods responsible for many different beliefs and understandings. The most dangerous of all God-like formations occurred when manmade God within his own image, imbuing God with human qualities like himself. With this act, man cursed his own image of God by imbuing it with his own selfish characteristics and qualities.

Moreover, this human-esque God affords man justification for destroying the world and permits man to commit evil acts throughout the world. Thus, this selfish, manmade God has become the most famous of all Gods. This God is not world-known because he harnessed the power of lightening, neither because he is a consummate mischief-maker nor because he is the most aesthetically pleasing to view. This God is the most famous of Gods because he sprang straight from man's ego in order to rule over all things. Man cannot even begin to conceive of the true Creator because his selfish ego will not allow him to do so.

Man deifies his selfish Gods through his practices based on selfish religions. Man glorifies his man-God in luxurious temples, accepting weekly down payments, in the man of the man-God, from the members of the congregation for a place in heaven, where they will live, with their manmade God, in peace and harmony forever and ever (the pie in the sky syndrome).

Because heaven is supposed to be the perfect state of life, I will attempt to show you that man's heaven is not where you want to go or be. First, man must free himself from this material world. This will allow the possibility of finding his true spiritual self. Once he finds his true self, man will begin to realize his true responsibilities to himself and to life. I think the Christians refer to this process as "being born again." Man must be reborn into the spirit of the natural vibration of Creation. At that point is where man connects with all that is.

Knowledge of love is founded on the belief that the Creator is the foundation of Love. It is due to this belief that most English speaking humans believe that their manmade Gods love them, which supports the idea that Gods loves everyone unconditionally and inclusively. This belief leads me to understand that any human being, creature or product of that Creator should have some of the characteristics, spiritual content and substance of the Creator. If humankind also believes this, then why do humans, especially English-speaking women, get so upset when they discover that their spouse or significant other loves another?

If the manmade God that this society teaches loves everyone is the true energy responsible for all of Creation, it seems to me that all humans should be able to love more than one person (mate, spouse) unconditionally. Contrary to popular belief, I believe they do. However and unfortunately, committing this act within this hypocritical society is considered wrong and a sin.

In fact, love, as practiced within our English-speaking society, defined mostly by selfishness and jealousy, stimulated by lust and physical desire to control. Man, as well as woman, gets married in order to control the physical existence of another human, commonly known as sex. Unfortunately, the spiritual presence is rarely considered. Now, just imagine if love was based primarily on the spiritual. There would be less strife, less divorce, less murders and fewer children left fatherless and motherless.

The only way the human can love unconditionally and unselfishly is to love based on the spiritual. The flesh is weak and is forever changing. The spirit is strong and resilient, and never changes. Even when absent of the flesh.

The human is become consumed with his ego and the ego is predicated solely on prejudice, selfishness and control. These negative energies have blinded so many humans worldwide that it is impossible to conceive any essence of true spiritual love.

Based on popular theological belief, humans sin by word, by thought and by deed. This theological tenet, upon occasion, mentioned within the church services of this society, but it is very rarely examined and these truths promoted sufficiently throughout this society for the statement to have a considerable and certainly not a lasting impression.

Nonetheless, the Creator is a loving existence and non-existence, spiritual and physical, tangible and intangible, both absence and presence, life and death. The Creator is all things that are good and positive.

The human is selfish. We only relate good to only those things that satisfy our selfish needs. The human can only see death in the tangible or physical absence. For the most part, humans relate 100% to the physical and psychological (reason and motive) to support the physical existence. Rarely is the spirit correctly perceived as the life source, and afforded the respect and the appreciation for being the energy that stimulates every function of life. Humans perceive spirit, rather, as a belief, as a myth or as something phenomenal. For the most part, humans rely on science.

Extension of Life

It has been said and thought, since time immemorial, that the first responsibility of Creation is production or procreation, for without this order and the fulfillment of said responsibility, life would not be. Life is supported by love, not by selfishness or hate. In order to express appreciation for this order, the human must be the energy that always loves existence and that promotes the extension of life. All of Creation honors that responsibility, AUTOMATICALLY. Any living thing that goes against that process interferes, stagnates or stops the life cycle.

Can a man favor a man over a woman and can a woman do the same? Yes! Yet still honor the procreative process? Yes, but only if neither he nor she is consumed with only the pleasure of sex, which is an egotistical emotion. The Ego interfered with that process when it created the word monogamy.

Monogamy only allows humans one mate, subject to civilization. Just envision, as best you can, a society that lacks monogamy but that promotes multiple mates, wherein a human being will be free to express himself or herself freely and still have their responsibility to human production/procreation met.

What is strange about all the fuss concerning man's feelings toward another man is that most men spend most of their time with men and the same goes for women. Now we must ask ourselves why it is nowadays that we translate these feelings into same-sex relationships as often as we translate them into natural heterosexual relationships. This understanding and acceptance of sameness is a deception of the ego because homosexual mating cannot bring forth life.

Just imagine if every human and everything desired to engage in same-sex relationships. There would be no future for life on this planet, certainly not in the sense that secular life could be observed and appreciated as it is today.

Two Types of Natural Love

In life, there are only two types of natural love. The first kind of love comes with the natural embodiment of Creation. This is the vibration that brought forth all that we know in our human existence. How do we know this? Because anyone who has ever lived life and committed themselves to all or to most of its elements knows that evil, which is the opposite of love, is committed and relegated to destruction. It does not take a rocket scientist to figure that much out. All you one has to do is to look around them. The lack of love has been and is the reason for the confusion and destruction we are experiencing today. The chaos is evident on every level of every organized society around the world. What the world truly need is love.

The second kind of love is Romantic Love. This is only a modification of natural love. I compare it to a black cup of coffee. It is the human quest to complete itself in the natural vibration of Oneness. This mission is diverse and can be confusing, based on ones social and environmental construct. Some can accept the black coffee just like it is while others need one lump of sugar. Others need more and more sugar and cream.

In the natural laws of life, love is beyond stigmatization, beyond limitation, so it cannot be relegated solely to marriage. Yet, in human social behavior, practicing love freely is considered an abomination. Society therefore promotes the practice of social marriage that, for the most part, is in many ways a hindrance to the natural vibration of Love. It often destroys family and tribal love. It takes humans away from the basic principles and values that nurtured them from birth to a sociological understanding of environment and self.

The Numerical System and Zero

The Creator's should always be represented with the numerical symbol zero. Why? Zero has no value system therefore, it is outside of time. Both Creator and zero are beyond limit. Free from shape, from size, from color, from any of the prejudices and barriers of the ego. The closest the human can get to an understanding or a picture of what this spiritual existence would be like is an animal in the wild. The Ego's influence extends to our human concept of this part of life, too. Man has exerted great influence in all parts of creation and on all levels of nature because of our selfish desires.

One represents the break or separation from the spiritual existence. It also represents the beginning of the ego's selfish mission. Its mission is to locate as many weak souls as possible in order to deceive them. The ego's campaign is to convince the weaker soul that more is better. The more toys and material their gain, the less the human will have to depend on God.

The ego has no life source of its own. It merely uses the human, whose source is God. This fact it cleverly conceals, diligent in its commitment to never allowing its followers to learn of or to rely on the true loving God of universal Oneness. Its reasons for keeping the human from the true Creator should be obvious. The ego wants you to believe in its Gods, the ones that the material minds pray to for their material toys, gadget blessings and a variety of pleasure-spawning treasures, while millions go without and die from all forms of deprivation.

Gods who have no love or mercy for the masses, only for a select group. The ego's Gods are prejudiced, selective and selfish. All of which is capricious and deceptive. The ego is always waiting, watching, for the weakness, for the opportunity to sneak into the soul of the human, without any regard for the human's spiritual needs. This is why so many humans who seem to have everything feel so empty. No. Spiritual fulfillment is something that the ego cannot give.

Products of the Ego

Everything produced by the ego has a monetary or material value. This egotistical value system starts with the birth of the human. Unfortunately, it does not stop there. This diabolical process touches and affects every human and everything comprehensively, forcing its selfish controlling system, wherever it exists. That is everywhere. It has little or no consideration for the less fortunate or for those without. Everybody has to pay some dues for love, God, birth, social acceptance and progress, health, and death. Nothing is without a price. This value system and the price you must pay let us know clearly that it is not of the true loving God of Creation. This system is owned and controlled by the Super Egos, and its mission is to show the true God that it can build a bigger, better and faster world, as well as control the universe.

This Egotistical mission is nowhere close to being achieved, but there have been technological advancement made, after a very ambitious start. At present, we do know they are already selling property on the moon, which means that the Super Egos, if they achieve their mission in outer space, they will do the same thing they have done here on Earth. They will carry the same rules, laws and prejudices, their selfishness and their monetary systems with them, therefore creating the same negative earthly conditions on the moon.

A Priceless World

Can you imagine a world without a monetary price tag? I am certain that to the contemporary human mindset, this image is quite difficult to conceive, except, of course, when we look back into history.

When we examine our past, we find that early man lived in societies without monetary mindsets. The method they used was to exchange a service for a service. They called it the barter system. Bartering lasted for many centuries.

This collective effort and willingness to accept service in exchange for service (as opposed to money in exchange for service) demonstrates that early man was much more loving than is today's man, and better equipped to accept his responsibilities to self, to his environment and to those he loved

All of Nothing

The Creator is total unification: all that can be conceived or imagined, and even all that you cannot imagine. The Creator is a state of absolute nothingness, without meaning, label or value.

Creation was a state of absolute Oneness but the intention of creating balance allowed choice, and with choice came desire. Hence began the Ego's journey away from the original creative order. Because the Ego has no life source of its own, it must carry the original creative spirit of life with it. The number two exposes, to the spiritually inclined, the Ego, despite its attempts to establish its own direction and autonomy, in its attempt to deceive Creation into accepting that more is better. In consideration of and by exploring the Ego's vain deceptions designed to convince mankind that it is better than God, I believe that I can I explain why it is that we have so many religions, churches and beliefs today, though the majority of these institutions claim that theirs is the true way to worship a single God.

The illusion of more has never been better and can never be. History proves this. Simply stated, the more you get the more you want despite the understanding that humans have destroyed themselves, and parts of Creation, trying to achieve this end. Nevertheless, the human Ego is determined not to give up or to give in, until either the person infected by Ego surrenders completely to it or until the Ego destroys itself.

The Ego would like for its system a mathematical time line for conquest to extend from 2 – 10. However, because it has no life source of its own, it must carry God's original loving creative spirit with it at all times. This is aggravating to the Ego. It must also include the true God with everything that it does. Therefore, instead of its equation and conquest timeline being from 2-10, the timeline must be from 1-10. Ten is the place where the Ego found a perfectly deceptive balance with the number five, which gives humanity two gods: one spawned by the Ego, which gives increasingly more beautiful toys to play with verses the actual God of the absolute unified and loving Oneness. This example gives us an understanding of why it is so hard to appreciate today.

The Ego, to date, has created its own selfish system wherein it plays social, materialistic games. Ego plays these games with humanity and with things like social survival, an example of which is acquiring the right mate or the right job. In addition, along with all that the Ego gives, the human always has the choice to return to the original creative order. This the Ego fears because without the human, the ego would have nothing.

All of nothing is nothing. All of something is nothing. This reality has been proven time after time, throughout life. Yet, of all of life's stories, the one that stands out the most, at least to me, is the story of Howard Hughes. He was a man who had everything but, in his final days, all of that something meant nothing to him. Still, the masses have nothing and desire to have something. Nevertheless, the misery of nothing is the same at the point of something. It means the same thing for both parties. It means simply nothing.

In our mathematical equation, nothing is presented by the lowest number, zero. In the spiritual equation, zero represents absolute balance: from nothing, all things were created. Nothing was labeled or had meaning. It simply was. This utopia did not last long because the unconditional spirit of love allowed choice. From choice sprung desire and the Ego was formed. The Ego labeled, it named, and it claimed everything in Creation. The Ego even formed its own mathematical system. It is a system of instigating itself into the lives of human beings. Instead of the human living only with the true God of loving Oneness, the Ego has created a space for itself by attaching itself to the human.

In the Ego's mathematical scale, one to ten, there is only one odd number that gives equal balance and that number is five. No other odd number enters ten equally, allowing us two, outside of five. Five enters the numerical scale of life and it allows two choices, both of which seem to be equal (at least in appearance), but life teaches the spiritually minded that the result of the two choices are not the same.

As I told you at the beginning of this chapter, the Ego is deceptive. If the number zero represents absolute balance, which is the true loving God of Oneness, then why is it that at the end of the Ego's life scale, the number one is in front of the number zero? Number one enters the scale first because the Ego was the first to leave God's original order and, over time, its influences have been devastating and extremely destructive.

On the Ego's scale of life, all equal numbers are perfectly balanced. For instance, the core number in all off numbers is equal. The equal numbers should always be a reminder of God's original order, which is where the Ego gets its life. It has no other life source. This is the reason why it, the Ego, works so hard to keep you under its control. It needs you. You do not need it. Over time, however, the Ego has tried to create and to invent its own life source, all to no avail.

All numbers, from one to nine, with the exclusion of zero, represents a human's Egotistical, physical plan or mindset. Zero is the greatest fear of the Ego. It works endlessly not to be recognized as nothing. The Ego sees no value in perfect balance, wherein everything is the same. Why not? Because there is no room for a controlling game herein. The Ego must have conditions and situations in which it can pose one human against another. This is the only way that it can have absolute control forever.

All of nothing is nothing and all of something is nothing. The reality may seem crazy or make no sense to the materialistic mind. But it has been proven throughout life, time after time. Maybe not on a large universal scale, but often on smaller scales. When all humans have equally the same things, having more or being better than, hardly or never enters the equation.

Of all of life's stories, the one that stands out the most, to me, is the life of Howard Hughes, a man who had everything yet to who, in his final days, all of his something meant nothing. With all the money and the power that he had, he could not find true spiritual love. This was only due to his materialistic application and commitment to life. He had blocked it out completely. He simply could not find his way back to his spiritual self. But, what is more interesting to me is that, even after his life story had been told, most people still desire to live his life. Having the all of something, not ever realizing that, in this materialistic world, the mystery of having something or nothing in reality is all the same.

If a man has nothing he wants more. If a man has all of something, he still wants more. More of what? He wants more of those materialistic things that he has little or no control over, things that will last only for a short time, never ever considering or even thinking about his spiritual self, which is the only true everlasting part of his existence. This part of us requires so much less to maintain than the toys we work so hard and die trying to acquire. Yes, Humans are interesting creatures.

The mindset or idea of having nothing is what they fear the most in this materialistic world and they will do anything, at any given time, in order to have something, and that something, at any given time, can change, based on conditions and circumstances.

Nothing in this materialistic world is represented by the number zero. Then, I really do not know whether I should consider zero a number. Only because all numbers from one to nine represent something and zero represents mere bliss or nothing. A place where Ego fears and never wants to be. Considering the valueless-ness yet importance zero, numbers are just another game of the Ego. It is extremely capricious and committed to keeping you off balance. The Ego is committed to giving you what you think you need and want, and then it leaves you when you are without. Now you are alone to find your way back to your spiritual self that you lost connection with and that you no longer recognize. Alone, to be supported by a Super Ego, that exerts even more control over you. These Super Egos become your Egotistical Gods, heroes and icons. Henceforth, you are enslaved for life.

True Love

The closest man comes to true love is his romantic idea of falling in love, which does not last very long. Often times, falling in love last only for a moment. Consider the great love stories as promoted within this society. Popular movies, television shows and novels capture moments of love, detailing the act of falling in love, but how many movies actually have a timeline of more than a day, a weekend, a week or a season?

Now imagine experiencing the feeling of falling in love. That feeling is what true love feels like, all the time, and without the stress of effort. It just is. Being in-tuned with love is being in tuned with nature and with the harmonies of Creation. It is a state of existence where everything is all right.

If you would like to know the condition that the world is in today, just imagine how it feels to fall out of love and having to wear that feeling everyday for the rest of your life.

True love is unlike a conqueror who peddles the ideas of love and concern only to take over a people, in order to change their way of life and their culture. True love never changes, it only supports. Love allows everything its own evolutionary right to change. True love never forces or manipulates.

Everything should be able to recognize true spirituality. It exists in all living things. True love is the origin of everything. A supportive energy that never leaves. You can leave it and you can try to forget about love, but it will never leave or forget about you. It is always there.

The reason most people cannot recognize love is that they have been consumed by the Ego. Ego creates its own selfish love, based on its own selfish reasons. Ego's love is consistently supported by Other Egos in its midst. Once Ego is supported by the other Egos, the games of compromise, manipulation and lying begin.

True Light

The only true light is life. With life, the human does not necessarily need eyes to see, though eyes are convenient and makes it easier to function on this physical plane.

The Miracle and the Energy of Love

I do not believe in commercializing love. Love to the human being is like electricity to the light bulb. When love lights you up, you should shine for the benefit of the whole world.

In this world, that usually feels loveless, your heart can grow weak and your load becomes too heavy to bear. Then a smile, like the gentle sweet air, appears out of nowhere.

I hope you can feel it, because I am sending it to you.

The energy of love is innocent and positive. It has no desire or need for negative or destruction. Like an infant, love is naked and is completely free of ego.

What Parents Should Teach Their Children

Children should learn that their parents are simply human vessels, produced by creation. Children should then learn that their creative responsibility is to bring forth, to extend and to care for human life, for the glorification of creation.

Material Verses Spiritual

The material world reminds me of a children's bedtime story, "The Three Little Pigs," wherein two pigs built houses of twigs and straw which is similar to the way in which the majority of people I have encountered within the past 20-years erect their inner spiritual sanctuaries: quick, fast and in a hurry, using left-over and often well-worn materials. The structures may even appear to be sound, as did the twig and straw houses of the pigs but neither the fairy tale stick houses nor the spiritual sanctuaries of most people I've encountered last very long.

According to the tale, the third pig built his structure out of stone, solid and strong, and he worked steadily. The stone structure represents the spirit of love. Love is the strongest force in the universe. It endures all things, even evil.

A problem with many of these people I have met within the past 20-years is that they want to own and to control love, but they cannot because love is a free spirit, freely bestowed upon humanity and freely accessible to all who seek it. Love cannot be owned or regulated.

This is the main reason little black boys and little white girls are loving and are marrying each other around the world today, actions once deemed miscegenation that would prompt immediate police response, incarceration and, too often, death. To allow oneself to enter into an interracial marriage is one example of achieving universal oneness.

Do you Believe in Heaven?

The traditional understanding of heaven is a place where God lives. A place you have no worries, unconditional love, endless harmony, no sickness, and no pain. Some believe it is a place of lakes of milk and honey while others believe that heaven is a place where many virgins await their arrival.

These beliefs come from the idea that God should or will reward them for living a decent and respectable life here on Earth. My question is why should God or anyone else have to reward any person for living a decent life for himself or herself? After all, it is their life! Live it as you wish and deal with the rewards, pleasures or consequences as you live.

Man is so selfish that he never includes the other animals in the heavenly rewarding ceremony. He reserves heaven for the chosen ones, meaning humans, and no other life form. Even more interesting is that with all that has been given to the perfection of his heaven, man is not anxious to go there. Man does everything medically possible not to go to heaven. He does everything he can to stay here on Earth, for as long as he can.

Man will not assume the responsibility of showing more than one way of getting to heaven, a heaven he created for the purpose of promoting fear and control. Instead, he hides behind the word of God. Man hides behind his false God because he does not want to accept his own imperfection. Man wants all of humanity to believe that the only way to get to heaven is through death.

Heaven is a state of spiritually loving Oneness and tranquility, when you are at peace with all of creation.

What is Knowledge

That which supports the complete unification and embodiment of Oneness, based on love, and only love, for love is the true knowledge. It is a feeling. A vibration. The same vibration that formed the universe and all that is within. It is the only true communication system.

False and artificial is all information not based on love. It only promotes confusion, separation, selfishness, and greed. It only fosters artificial intelligence.

The human is a spiritual being embodied in a temple of flesh. This is not today's popular understanding: the human is a physical being with a spirit. The spirit that today's society knows of is the energy of the Ego. The Ego has taken humans from natural law, which is governed by the loving vibrations of the universe.

The Father, Son and the Holy Ghost

The Father gives the recognition and the appreciation of living called life. The Son is all who are procreated from life. The Holy Ghost is the energy that holds all of Creation intact. The human being does not create life, neither can it give life. It knows nothing about life. It only knows a fraction of procreative life. Man knows nothing about the origin of life or about life, period. He has many theories but none is factual.

Even with the most intelligent and sophisticated mind, man does not understand life, yet he cannot deny that life allows procreation in all forms. Even when, in his limited understanding, life has expired, life continues to procreate. After all, man only understands tangible life: that which he can see, feel or touch. He is ignorant concerning the origin of life.

Even though man has harnessed the elements and other components of life, he has never been able to capture life nor to control it. To his dismay, he will always be subject to the natural rhythms of life and always left to wonder about his own existence, regardless of whether he is rich or poor, good or bad, right or wrong. Life makes all of us equal and relative because we all are connected to the same source. Life. Just life. Life created man. Man cannot create life.

The God Chapter

God is the total embodiment of nothing, consisting of all you need in order to be, supporting you with the energy we have labeled as true love. Love is that energy waiting to accept you when you have divested yourself of want and return to nothing. You will, too, when you have all that you desire and wanted and you realize that it means nothing.

The Lap

Where does the lap go when you stand up? The same place all other negative, brainwashed programs go. Hence, man becomes his own creative self.

When he stands up and becomes his own man, he realizes that he has been conditioned and forced to believe all the negatives that have prevented him from being. Man.

The Value of Man

Ask any man how much he is worth. Right away, the material mind kicks in and he thinks of himself in a material way. He places a price on himself. However, within seconds, the spirit overrides the ego and he says "priceless." This is how all humans feel about themselves. Priceless.

Proves that what was originally created to be a loving spiritual existence has become an artificially materialistic hell in man's hands. The single most important part of the human existence is the spirit. Every human must know that once the spirit leaves the body, it is over for the physical body. Yet it is hardly talked about or thought about and is always second to the material world.

Sex

Coming from a small town in the South to the big city of Philadelphia, PA was quite a cultural shock for me. At the time of my arrival, I was only seventeen years old, naïve, ill exposed, and I had very little experience with sex. Yet I was wide open and eager to learn. With many popular male relatives already living in Philadelphia, it was not difficult for me to meet and to get involved with females: all ages, sizes, complexions, and nationalities. The more females I got involved with the more I learned about sex. Moreover, I was enjoying every minute of it. It was one of the most exciting times of my life. I was having lots of sex.

At one point in my life, I thought of myself as a sex addict, which, in reflection, was not a good thing. Nevertheless, at the time, I was having a good time. The foremost thing I realized was that girls were much more aggressive than I believed. Sometimes they would even approach me, initiating the sexual seduction.

This lifestyle was quite different from any I had learned to anticipate, having been raised in the South where some mothers and fathers would have cringed with disbelief and shock if they had thought that their sons and daughters were even thinking this way. Sometimes I myself was shocked and surprised by what girls would do in the privacy of hotel rooms or in the dorm rooms of college campuses.

Some of the sexual acts I engaged in were crazy, extreme to the norm and over the edge. I was amazed at how far a female would go to obtain sexual satisfaction. These sexual encounters became so easy and common that the original thrill and excitement were no longer there. Therefore, I started experimenting.

At this point, every sexual tryst became an intensely observed encounter. I closely watched the motions and vibrations of the female bodies to see how they reacted to my penetration and applications. The more I experimented and observed the more I begun to realize that there was more to the act than just the big thrill, masculine empowerment and general excitement.

I began to realize that there was something spiritual about the thing called sex. The more I committed myself to the spiritual side of this act, the more mysterious and mystical this act became.

I began to ask myself what is it that makes women endure extreme pains and tortures for the sake of sexual gratification. I started to feel that something had to be wrong with our approach to this act called sex, even considering that I had once enjoyed sex just for the sake of sex, not truly caring about the females' interests. Back then, it was all about me satisfying my masculine ego, as I had been taught: "get as much as you can."

Moreover, I had done just that. I had gotten my share and more: unappreciable reputation and attitude. I continued to explore and to discover as much as I can about the spiritual side of sex. One of the first things I realized is that I did not like the title "sex" anymore. I started to feel more as if I was mating. It was a coming together of a spiritual oneness with more than just a physical, egotistical function.

The act referred to as "sex" in this society is actually a human sacrifice and a spiritual commitment to allow another life form into this world. The more involved I become in my spiritual commitment to discovering self the more I understand that sex is a sacred act. It should not be forced, purchased, abused, taken for granted, or sold.

Mating should be the spiritual vibration of two bodies coming together to procreate life. The pleasure, joy and excitement that come along with procreation process bespeak total spiritual enjoyment and oneness.

As practiced within this society, sex is a diabolical exploitation of what should be the most spiritual union between male and female, animals or plants. It should be the process of bringing forth new life, for the extension and glorification of life.

Man has separated the natural spiritual union from the male and the female. He did this by placing value on the human reproductive organs. Man has valued female organs higher than male's. He changes this value system whenever he wants. A system used to control the men who are not in control. A system that deprives these disadvantaged of a natural God given pleasure' a pleasure that promotes joy. Happiness. Life. Oneness.

Sex means deception, competition, separation, sneaking, lying, bargaining, and sometimes death, all of which are definitely products of the Ego.

Today we have men and women bargaining back and forth, trying to determine how much their organs are worth from moment to moment, on this day or whenever they get the feeling. They bargain with any and everything from a simple smile to millions of dollars for this natural, glorified pleasure.

Man's selfish economical system dictates what kind, what social status and which nationality of woman with whom he can have sex. This act of abuse, deprivation and separation creates a negative energy called desire. Desire for that which he wishes for but knows or believes he cannot have. Yet, he feels a natural closeness to all women, regardless of how they are or where they come from.

Some men become intensely committed to all kinds of heinous, vile, diabolical acts when denied healthy sexual expression. Then the Super Egos prosecute these men, using the same system that caused these conditions to arise in the first place. Women suffer the same abuses from the Super Egos as men. The only difference is that, collectively speaking, women did not create this system, men did. Sometimes, the hunter is caught by the game.

Education

Those who advocate teaching have but one understanding. The only way to teach a human being is first, to teach him to love and to appreciate self. Second, teach him to understand body, his mind and, above all else, his spirituality. Third, teach him the ways in which he can bring the three preceding components of himself together, as one, to better manipulate his entire environment for his own survival, and for the survival of others. Finally, fourth, make sure that he understands that he is not responsible for his own existence.

You Have Been Screwed!

Why don't we take Mother Nature and father time seriously? The rewards and the benefits are for our pleasure. Why not? Because we are taught, from our beginning, to be abusive. Yes, you too have been screwed!

The way back to your loving spiritual self is everyday commitment to acts of love. Sit on a park bench, watching and listening to birds sing. Watch the squirrels play or just hug a tree.

The Quest for Absolute Control is Evil

The suppression of natural free will creates all negative social conditions and all negative energy. Nothing in Creation concerns itself with the reasons why it was created or why anything else is created, except the human.

The whys of Creation will never be answered, yet the human continues, endlessly, trying to figure it all out: lying, pretending, deriving theories based on facts that are constantly being altered. Why? Because there are no absolute answers.

Many stories have been told to frighten or to convince, all done in an effort to exalt the human Ego. The Ego will never control love, which is the force that holds Creation together.

"There is nothing new under the sun," Ecclesiastes 1:9. Creation is self-contained, self-reliant and self-supported. Creation is perfect, needing nothing but to be left alone and appreciated.

The closer a human is connected to the energy of "the first separation", meaning the original choice to separate from the natural, unified, spiritual, unlabeled, unvalued, loving order of Creation, the more the human is committed to and desires to hold on to this selfish, diabolical, separative order, controlling and destructive though it is. This energy is passed down from one generation to another, but the beauty of the Creative energy (which is love) is that it is unconditional, committed only to love. It never leaves the Ego or the Super Ego. It is always there, as a reminder to the Ego that the road on which to return to the original order is still there. The Ego would only need to surrender its mission to conquer, to control, to destroy, and to separate in order to be reunited with oneness.

Existence Cannot Be Measured

If the Ego decided to measure it, then in time "something" lasts only a short time, compared to the measurement of "nothing". Nothing will always be there, waiting for something to surrender to it. It has waited and it always will.

For example, if I gave you something, would you treat it as nothing or would you honor the energy that motivated the act of giving? Would you, perhaps, honor the something itself and forget about the motivating energy? Would you honor the gift or the energy that motivated and sustained the giving of the gift?

Doubtful that the latter would be true because true love is always taken for granted. Why? Because it is always with you and with all of Creation. True love lasts forever, like all that is a part of the natural order. Things of the Ego last for only a short time. Unfortunately though, the Ego never stops. It always has something new with which to taunt you. Taunting creates friction and a sense of scarcity. These false energies promote desire.

Desire is a state in which the Ego wants all of Creation. This is the state wherein the Ego has complete control. Desire is a state wherein the human can never have enough toys to play with. So much so that human beings will sacrifice themselves, fight wars and destroy entire nations in order to keep their toys.

The Ego is afraid of nothingness. It cannot survive without something. The Ego is the complete opposite of the true essence of God, wherein all of Creation just is---no labels, no titles, no values, and no meaning. Just is.

God is Life and Life is the Only God

The Creator is powerful energy with the ability to transform Itself into all things. This is an undeniable fact. Why? Because all things are, and all things that are the Creator is responsible for, including the mind that allows a human to wonder about It.

To present this fact more palatably, all things with life are connected to life. Creation is creation, life is life. However, man named, defined, separated and placed value on all things for his own selfish control and benefit.

God is Not Loving, God is Willing

The will just to do verses "Do I love you enough to." The human has been programmed, via civilization, to look for and to appreciate only certain qualities in other humans and within the spectrum of Nature. To believe that the human's selective love is the Creator's will in play and that the former can help to develop a productive and harmonious world is more than a foolish notion, it is anti-Christ.

A willing giver and a willing receiver are the only humans in tune with God's Creative order. No conditions allowed.

Please bear in mind that there is no sin. Nature will die and will recreate or correct itself and then continue onward.

Why

Why am I Black? Why am I what they say I am? Am I? Who are they to say who and what I am?

Why is Black black? Is it just a color? Is it the absence of light? Is it the absence of knowledge? Why, if Black is a color, am I not as Black as the color?

Why am I White, when I am not like the color white? Is White the absence of color or is it a metaphor for light? Does White indicate the content of knowledge?

Why, if God made man and woman, are there boys and girls? Why not just grown man and women, growing further into maturity?

Why am I a human being instead of a spiritual vessel, when we know that the body is nothing without the spirit?

Why can't we love ourselves completely? Why are we taught to separate ourselves and to love only certain parts? Why is the head, the organ housing the brain, less important (judging by our current social value system) than the buttocks? Especially in light of the reality that one is exalted to the air and heavens, literally, due to its placement, while the other is covered and spends most of its uncovered time atop a commode. The commode, a place, by the way, where most humans would not put any other part of their body, a place that prompts parents, even today, to withhold allowances they normally provide to their children, provided the children have not thoroughly scoured that area before the daily or weekly chore inspection?

Why is gold more valuable than wood when we get more benefits from the wood?

To fulfill means to give to that which has no Godly spiritual substance some Godly spiritual substance. Man has always been given the knowledge to address the preceding inquiries and all others, but man's selfish ego has consistently mis-used the knowledge for its own gain.

The Three Dimensions of Man

From the beginning of the human's Egotistical consciousness, the human being has been a wonder to himself. "What am I" or "who am I" are the questions man has asked. Well, considering my own life experiences and my observations of life, of nature and of its functions, the answer to these questions is simple. Man is an existence, a mere creature, an animal, a phenomenally organized piece of flesh with a responsibility to life and to its continuance, whether man believes that he originated from a piece of clay of the earth, some gelatinous mass from the sea or a conglomerate of elements that have manifested via osmosis. It simply does not matter. He, as he has himself claimed, exists.

Could man, after identifying and separating himself from all other portions of creation, just exist? No. Man would then have to find a support system within his midst to support his separation from all that has been created. And, as we should all know by now, even if the only thing we can conceive of being separate from is, say, our own mind (the greatest recorder ever created, by the way) chaos would quickly ensue.

There has always been a force opposing the loving oneness and, if we are fair to ourselves and honestly submit to the energy of love, we can admit how very difficult it is to give consistently while failing to receive. I am not talking about anything materialistic here. Just love.

Many have asked why love is so difficult to give when it does not cost a thing. Well, man, very early in his life process, found a support system called Ego. The Ego support system allows man to be bigger and better or anything else, as long as it is in opposition to the loving oneness, which is God.

The more man separated and the bigger he became in that of his Ego, the more he experienced complications and difficulties, situations that his Ego will not allow him to figure out, completely. For example, the ability to clearly answer the "where did I come from?" question. Man has many theories and hypotheses but he is not now nor will he ever be satisfied with a single answer until he surrenders his Ego and submits to unconditional love. This is the only path he can take to understand that which he cannot understand. The only way that he can surrender his Ego is to abandon it and then submit to the Loving oneness.

To the spiritually founded and committed, most of the mysteries of life have been revealed. For the most part, this understanding is quite simply: Why so? Because, the spiritual mind has always observed life forms manifesting from what is considered nothing or simply waste. I have known this fact for most of my life. For example, the emergence of life from a pile of rotten fruit, from garbage or from stagnate water. Life is a mystery and it will continue to be one for those curious minds that want to know their beginning and what God looks like.

Why does it matter? Why feel compelled to "see" the Creator? The fact that you exist, whether in mind, flesh or spirit. You exist. Work with that and with whatever started the ball to rolling, whether it is single or plural, it is God or your Creator.

There have been times I thought man must have been created from a pile of monkey feces, based on the games we play, which are, far too often, very destructive or fatal. We chase our tails as if we have yet to realize that it is part of the whole body. Laughing, grinning, and jumping around, as if life is one big joke.

The jumping up and down? The anticipation? Well, let's introduce the taunting of a commercial, which is not simply a TV commercial, but is actually the social indoctrination of another toy, another play thing which, ironically, plays with our minds more than we can play with it (the toy).

Television commercials come in many different forms: verbal, fashionable, political, economical, theological, etc., but they are always coming, all with a single intent. Commercials are designed to keep the human being off-balanced and filled with a sense of heightened desire, to ensure that the viewers never glimpse the reality that they do, in fact, have enough. Moreover, commercials deceive their viewers into accepting the idea that they can have wholesome and fulfilling lives by merely entertaining their flesh, never signifying that in order for a human being to have a wholesome life, they must entertain their spiritual side. Commercials promote the neglect of spirituality, that part of a human which is most important and without which there would be no human.

In today's media-infatuated American culture, there is constant chatter about financial stimulus, and how its use will break the backs of the working people. You know the "earn your bread by the sweat of your brow" syndrome. Because the Ego plays both sides, it is difficult for most people to see or to recognize the game that is being played, especially concerning the poor and the needy. The Ego has always introduced and given stimulus to humanity, in one way or another, from destructive stone instruments to technological machines. As much as it has appeared to help, it has done significant damage, damage directed at breaking the natural spiritual will of humanity.

I am not saying that some good things have not been done, but for all the wrong reasons. Just as committed as our international society has been to greed, to profit and to control, it could just as easily also have been committed to love, to sharing, and to universal oneness. Man's refusal to accept the loving Oneness is taking him on a mission of total human destruction only because he refuses to surrender his Ego and submit to love. To the intellectual and Egotistical mind, man makes up the second component of the trinity. You know, the three-in-one concept, which is a very common understanding. However, what does it mean?

The term trinity refers to the Biblical concept of three as one: the Father, son and Holy Ghost. So there you are. A definition, but no one I know, read about or have ever met can authenticate its origin. The concept of the trinity is merely an ideological component that is well promoted, one that many Christians have accepted and believe in. Moreover, no person should have the right to persecute him or to try to stop him from believing. When he is ready, each man will realize that he must believe in something, if no more than in himself. In this, man has no choice. Love will not allow him to exist without beliefs.

Love has never left the Egotistical man, even in as much as he has tried to leave love, love has always been there and it always will be. Intrinsically, all humans know this yet they ignore this or take this fact for granted. Why? Especially since we know, we truly have control over nothing, not even our own bodies.

Bodies function at their own rhythm and vibration, whether we acquiesce or not. The only way these bodily functions do not occur is when the body is diseased or otherwise impaired, which proves that true love is unconditional and always supportive. Even to the consumed and Egotistical human mind and body, the latter a vessel whose fate you believe that you control.

The Christian faith speaks of the Trinity as a three-in-one head, placing the Father first. Yet, what has been revealed to me, as I travel along my spiritual journey, is that love is first. Why not, considering that it is the most powerful energy in the universe. A mustard seed of love can move a mountain; bring forth vegetation from a slab of concrete, etc. In light of this, then, could love not also have brought forth a father and a son?

Love, father and son are the Trinity I believe in, which are the three dimensions of man. This is how it was revealed to me. Love is first, father is second and son is third. Love is the only thing, even today, that has not changed. A resounding vibration is heard, felt, recognized, and needed by people around the world. Humans long for it, beg for it, pray for it, and die for it. It is a vibrant feeling and expression that is welcomed and received universally, whether you know the language and culture of the person giving love or not. This vibration is awesome, devastating and powerful. I identify it as the Holy Ghost.

In my social experience, I have not found or experienced anything more miraculous than the Holy Ghost. For those readers who feel they have no foundation for understanding how love looks or how it might feel, they should think of a tree or a newborn baby because love has no form, shape or size. It is a resounding vibration that can only be felt.

The father, I believe, is the spiritual manifestation of what I now know as the Creator, void of Ego, indignities, rights or wrongs. The Creator, subject only to love and committed to Creation, for the glorification of life. The Creator is the total unification of all things.

The son is a manifestation of all that came before him, a combination of love, spirit and the physical. At a period in his existence, the son could transform, at will, from spirit to physical, utilizing the gift of choice. The son shared the responsibilities of the universe with both the vibration of love and the father.

Man, as we have proclaimed ourselves, is a combination of all of the elements within the universe and the gift of choice, alien then, by virtue of his creation, to tiredness, weariness, doubt or desire. These descriptions cultivate vanity. When these unnatural states arose an were entertained sufficiently, they prompted man to deceive himself into believing that he should no longer be subject to the father or love. Man's choice was to separate, subject to his own will and power, finding his own direction, which has resulted in the conditions we have today.

Man separated from the spiritual realm, which left him in the physical form. Man no longer has the abilities he had before he separated himself from the spiritual realm. But, he did have the same responsibilities, as did all beings that followed man into the separated state. The being who proclaimed himself "man" is limited. He could not go forward as he had limited help tending to his responsibilities. Yet, as you have learned in this chapter, love is both awesome and unconditional. Love provided man a vessel full of love containing the seed of life. We know this second vessel as woman. Woman allowed man the ability to procreate and to bring forth being, like himself.

For all who are looking for complete peace and tranquility, it is not to be found in our future, for it is in our past. It was after the ninth cycle when the life process changed. If you notice, the numerical scale of life starts with 0-1 and ends with nine. After nine, it starts a new beginning with 10. This formulation gives the number one power over the zero when, in truth, zero represents complete balance. Zero is the order where both love and God exists, where all things are the same and where all things mean the same. Zero represents the union of God and love whereas one represents the son and all that was brought forth for his survival. Two represents man and God---man's first awareness of the Godhead. Three represents the Holy Ghost, God and man. Four represents one more than three and, if Love, God and man signify the perfect union, there is no need for any additional.

This extra one is the master taunter in its invasion of the holy trinity. It functions in trying to persuade man to go in the opposite direction. I believe that this number four is the point where both doubt and desire infected man. Five is the acceptance of the Ego, six is the first attempt to return to the original order, and numbers seven and eight represent total confusion. Number 9 was man's last true attempt to return to the original order.

After number nine, the Ego took control and it turned the natural order of existence around, placing itself before love and God. Five is where this started. Five goes into ten and fosters the two Gods that are necessary in order to address the Ego's selfish desires.

The Ego's main objective is to separate the original order of divine oneness, an order where everything is the same and everything has the same, a state governed only by the vibration of love. The greatest component of love is choice. It was choice that allowed the Ego to select its own way, with the support of love. We should all keep in mind that true love has no choice. It can only allow choice.

It was in the fifth cycle where this formerly supernatural being who today proclaims itself "man", submitted itself to its Ego and its destruction, separating itself from the realm of spirituality to create its own world, and I believe that the numerical scale from zero to ten represents this, with zero representing the loving Godly order (in the non-physical realm). One, then, represents man, an entity once empowered to transform self from physical to non-physical states and to travel through the universe at will, possessing all the powers and knowledge of its spiritual predecessors, to create and procreate. However, in his quest to separate from the loving order, man relinquished all of his supernatural abilities to his selfish, greedy, controlling, self-serving Ego. As you can see, the Super Egos are doing well for themselves today. Woe to the lesser Ego that foolishly follows in their wake.

Today's lesser Egos, as much as they have since the original separation occurred, but more noticeable today because nothing is hidden within this society, must work around the clock in order to compete with the God order. The Super Ego's committed mission and objective are to show all of humanity and the Creator that can do it all, only bigger and better that the loving order can. Yes, today the Super Ego can still fly through the universe at will, but on an airplane or spacecraft. For a price. It can still create and procreate. For a price. Ego's God will help to support you. For a price. You can unite with Ego's almighty God. For a price. If you are unable to pay the price, the Ego will gladly condemn you to his hell.

Again, the number five is a most deceptive number in that it signifies the consumption of man by his Ego. Number 10 is the false beginning and it is where the Ego gave humanity the proverbial cross (road), a system of mass confusion whereas, pre-separation, man had direct communication with the Creative head. Post-separation, though, man was forced to accept two Gods.

The first God he accepted because he had allowed desire to seduce him, leading him away from the spiritual realm, leaving him only his physical state. The explanation addresses the unasked questions concerning reasons why, in religious depictions of the Ego's cross or crossroads, the spirit ascends into the heavens or into the elements while the physical remains nailed to the cross. Actually, the cross is where man has been from the moment the separation occurred until the present time. This is why I believe that the number ten is the beginning of the false artificial system that we live today, a value system of greed, competition, destruction, deceit, and the beginning of the bigger-and-better syndrome.

You may well, by now, wonder how I arrived at this belief and understanding. Well, on my spiritual journey of life, these understandings have been revealed to me. As I have mentioned before in this chapter, zero represents the union of God and love. One only represents man. And as it was in the beginning of the human life numerical scale, zero was before one. After number nine, which represents man's third and final period of awareness and of affirmation, a false number appeared, and that number was 10. Ten is false only because it was the beginning turned around. Now the one is in front of the zero. The only reason the Ego did not rid itself of the number one (man) all together is because it has no life support of its own. So it hides, obscurely, in the mind (or soul) of humanity, leading man around like herds of cattle.

Man has forgotten the spiritual side of his existence. He treats it as if it is fantasy or just something to talk, argue, preach about, and make money off of. The true Creator of loving oneness is passé. Not quite exciting enough while the new God of bling-bling offers exciting toys and many tricks. It is your choice. You must decide whether it is the mush or the filet mignon (see the movie "The Matrix"). Always remember that the spirit of love has never left you. You have left the spirit. It is your choice.

You chose long ago and are choosing everyday whether to allow the Ego to trick and to beguile you or whether you will submit to the loving Oneness and return to your intended state. There are even ways to recognize the control that your Ego has over you.

I know you have asked yourself countless time questions along the lines of "who am I," "what am I," "am I just a servant, a slave of someone just to be used?" Yes! You are just that to your Ego. It cares nothing for you, only for itself. Your Ego rides, controls and uses you until you are old, weary and beaten down, if you are lucky. Then, it makes you pay, while you are dying, a death that it is responsible for. Unfortunately, that is the best that it does for you.

For many of its adherents, the Ego drives them straight to the nut house while it prods others into high-risk crime ventures where it (Ego) leaves them the second they are in trouble or about to be killed, often dying before they get the chance to understand who or what life is truly about.

For the record, let us think for a moment about the things we say, do and live-out daily, actions we cannot recall having originated with ourselves. Again, I am compelled to remind you that the spirit has never left you. It is always there, reminding the body of its natural functions. Have you ever stopped to ask yourself why you accept the title of man or woman, what those prescribed titles mean to you, personally, or why you do things to satisfy someone or something else outside of yourself?

Things, for the most part, do not satisfy your inner being, which is the spiritual self that you have been taunted and directed away from entertaining. Some call this inner self their first mind while others call it their subconscious mind, but for those who are trying to make the turn back to oneness, it is the spirit doing its job.

Have you ever noticed that, too often, people in relationships treat lovemaking as a job? They believe and try to practice, with their equally Ego-obsessed partners, that lovemaking has a prescribed time of the day or evening, and not freely participating when they actually feel the spiritual need to unite. Other life forms adhere to their spiritual procreative and lovemaking clocks Spiritually-instigated lovemaking could indeed be a time of conception of the child you have longed for but you waited until a time you thought (as opposed to felt) was right. Why? And, if not for the conception of a child, then a time to consummate your relationship with your loved one as a reminder of what you mean to each other. However, you waited. A moment later, you may have very well regretted the thought of having waited.

Moreover, why do you have to stay categorized, with a particular group, category, social strata, or nationality in order to find your soul mate? Why are most men taller and older than most women in relationships? Now ask yourself why you focus on such banality when a woman should be focusing on a man who is spiritually connected to love with wisdom and who knows how to survive inside and outside of his environment, for her and her entire family.

Now for the baby. Why can't the baby just be healthy spiritually, mentally and physically? Why must we have designer babies? It must have a particular eye color, a certain grade and texture of hair and must be a certain size and shape. Then we plan the child's life before they can walk or talk, hardly ever focusing on what a unique beauty nature has provided us or nurturing the child in that fashion. We go all out to satisfy the Ego. Man even tried to change the natural direction of human life in the embryonic stages. The madness does not end there, as man wants everything by design. Design only of the Ego.

Humanity is destroying itself at the direction of and submission to the Ego only because we refuse to follow the loving, divine spirit of the Creator. Love has always had this adversary, but because of man's weakness, the Ego has seduced man into submitting to it and following its direction to a state of Ego-infection. It seems that humanity is doomed. But I live in hope that one day man will get tired, sick and weary of its (the Egos) tricks and return to the loving oneness. We must submit to unconditional love in order to destroy the diabolical enemy that lives within our midst and, ultimately, within ourselves. Love is where the Ego cannot exist.

Why were you taught to eat unhealthy foods, foods that we have learned are killing us slowly, yet we continue to consume them? Why do we buy clothes we do not need and throw away perfectly good clothes? Because someone told us our clothes were out of fashion? This destructive list goes on endlessly, subject to the direction of Ego. Then there you are, with a noose of debt around your neck that you have grown comfortable being suffocated by. Sometime, you must ask yourself questions that, though painful, will enable you to see life in a different vein, i.e. why are you responsible for your own destruction at the expense of glorifying your Ego?

I have experienced a multitude of things in my life: ideas, theories, hypothesis, lies, scant truth, the need for love, a lot of hatred, deceit, war, life, and death, but nothing as consistent as the alphabet and number systems. I believe both of these systems have true spiritual substance, which does not negate the fact that both have been used to create much destruction. The latter point addresses the main reason why both systems have withstood the test of time and why they have been instrumental to human survival. I will attempt, herein, to use these two systems to provide a clearer understanding of how this thing called human life got started.

The sound, the vibration, the noise, or the utterance, whether aloud or silent. It is love that man needs and longs for. Humans have named this need and this feeling love. My experiences and observations of life have convinced me that this is the most powerful energy within the universe. Love is even responsible for the manifestation of the God we have claimed as our universal master. Many readers will, of course, frown on this assertion while others will not. I do understand.

Stop and think for a moment about sound, noise or whatever you believe the vibration to be. You must recognize the power of sound, not simply in one way, but in the many applications that it lends itself to: sound forms designs, crumbles mountains, causes floods and avalanches, unites people together and, often, the lack of sound forces people apart. Sound is vibration. Most of all, to humans, it is the number one component in the process of human procreation.

Even if humans do not love or like their partner, they love the mere idea of making love (intercourse). Love is powerful, a vibration heard, felt and needed around the world. Love is a resounding vibration that is larger and more powerful than Creation. It is, in fact, the only force that holds Creation all together.

The unique thing about love is that most people never think about it or talk about it. When most

Gods are not accepted outside of a particular culture, love is, and even to foreign, love is understood. As quiet as most men may keep it, most of them pray for true love in their solitude, afraid that if they expose this need to the Ego, they will be cut-off from their material world and then denied the honor, reverence and rewards they receive when being social, Egotistical dick heads.

The Ego, the Creator and Nothing

What is the Creator? The Creator is the beginning and the first spiritual formation of all that is loving and good, balance in oneness, void of Ego. The absence of thought. If you think about the Creator, It will become what you want it to be, not what it is. Nothing.

No value system, no right, no wrong, no beauty, no ugly, no big, no small, no short, no tall, no rich, no poor, no man, no woman, no jealousy, no hate. Its beginning started with love and with love it has no end. Love has no value system so that makes it nothing.

Nothing is the beginning of what the Ego has proclaimed as something, as desire is the belief that you do not have all that you need. Only the Ego measures and compares.

We live and we die, not for any real reason. Yet the Ego gives us many reasons. The Ego cannot respect Nothing. It must make it something, own it and then control it. Its number one method of control is separation, initially separating the spirit from the body that houses it.

Demons are super negative forces that come from the negative power of the Ego. This component of the demon comes from abuse, neglect, deprivation, ignorance, lies, false indoctrination, forced segregation, forced integration, sex, desire, and freedom. Demons are created when a person does not have the right to express him or herself freely, and, as a result, they suppress. The suppression creates the demon.

The size, the shape, the color, and the image of your demons are based on those Egos that came before you. Image does not matter, however, because all demons dwell within the realm of control. Can the Ego discover anything, create or invent anything, and share it equally? Absolutely not. Nothing that has been created can humans rightly claim as our own.

Where does the Ego come from? It just is. It is like all natural things of the natural order of choice. We could ask why we have air and where it comes from or why a raindrop fell in a particular spot, but why bother? Simply accept that it just happened.

Ego comes from the natural order of awareness, but the Ego will not accept the state of nothing. It must name, label and define in order to exalt its power and control. Ego comes from suppression of all the natural things. Any system outside of the natural order creates this energy of resistance, resisting all that is natural for its ownership.

Men who praise the Creator believe that the Creator has and will continue to give them what they want. Men who curse the Creator believe that It has disappointed them. The phrase "damn God" is currently as popular as "praise God."

Everything has a vibration and vibration ultimately becomes sound, noise, music, and utterances. Utterances become words. The Ego ultimately forms into tribal or/and national formal communication systems, owning and controlling the masses. The Ego only allows a few privileged the full understanding of the system. Communication is the most powerful force among humans. Words form how a human thinks of self, starting with the words man and woman.

No man wins his freedom. Man is allowed his freedom by those who control freedom, even though Creation made all things free. It was Ego that took away "free" and replaced it with "freedom."

Freedom means free but domesticated. Free to do what the controlling Ego allows you to do. All of these things support the creation of the demons within us all.

Man should live and accept life for what it is, just as we accept the seasons. For everything is in Creation. We receive both our negative and our positive, if we live. Yet, in terms of Creation, all is good.

Can we see, define or understand beyond what we have been taught? The energy called Spirit takes us beyond the human psyche into spheres that we do not understand and that we cannot recognize. Yet sometime, in time with time, we understand bits and pieces. It is only within our solitude where we get true understanding.

The worship of and submission to negative energy will create a negative reality, complete with living negative creatures that have the creative characteristics of the Creator. Negative attracts negative and positive attracts positive. Negative cannot hide from negative, not even within the sub mind. To lie to self is negative. Positive has no reason to hide for it can only be based on unconditional love. Religion is negative as it separates, destroys and lies. Sex is negative as is social love, marriage, economics, politics, segregation, and forced integration.

The beauty of Creation is accepting that all is nothing, thus without value. What happens when one no longer owns, controls or has any use for a thing? That thing has no value, but you wasted time and energy acquiring it.

The greatest punishment to humanity is confinement. This tactic is used on every social level: social segregation, economic disparity, religious ostracizing, prison (aka the Hole), educational lack, ignorance of basic communication systems, lack of housing, etc. Being confined means being cut-off from self and from the world in which one lives, only to heighten the control of another, which spawns (within the disenfranchised) the demonic process called desire. Desire without the knowledge or the means to achieve.

What type of mind would organize and structure a system that is dedicated to depriving the human being of knowing and of appreciating his own mind and body? Most humans are afraid to explore their bodies and, in some cases, are even ashamed of them. We have been given minds and bodies with a natural spirit, but the promoters who control the system have us behaving as if we radically different (physically and mentally) from every other human on the planet, which again serves to intensify demonic energy, this time called fear. This fear is extended to every level of human social life. Hence, the human body has become a lethal weapon.

Organized religion is a control system put in place by a person or persons for social direction and for absolute control. It is a drug, impairing the mind and which takes from reality, creating whatever fantasy and direction it wishes, inviting intense fear, false happiness and false pleasure. If I win, then the Creator is for me. If I do not It is against me.

To appreciate Creation for what it gives us is to support our survival. This is as natural as a baby appreciating the breast of the mother without the social importance of the breast. We are all eternal babies to Mother Nature and she will always have a nipple for us. Learn to appreciate it. The first step in this appreciation process is to understand love. Love is not worship. Worship is for idols, for something that does not last. Creation and love are forever.

Why should a mature and responsible man be forced by social mores to marry a woman who has, especially if reared within modern American society, been used, abused and grossly underappreciated? Especially in light of the prevailing practice, again, within modern American society, wherein unmannered and irresponsible boy-children are fathering children by these same girls (when the girls are still relatively un-jaded)?

The creative energy we call Love never leaves you, even in your resistance. Love is a free energy, creating everything free with free will. Rebelling for the sake of rebelling against someone else's Ego system is to put your own Ego in place, never realizing that, neither party within this scenario is seeking love. It is a mere Ego joust.

The Creator is the ultimate unification of all things and all things are nothing in It. There is no value system. Only the Ego needs labels and titles.

The death of the Ego is the resurrection of love. The energy of Ego influences the reproductive process in humans and all human value systems.

We live in a world of ever-changing values. There will always be someone who will be deprived or without something to value. Value changes with the whim of the Super Ego, which is the controlling, dominate power at any given time, in time. The Super Ego determines or decides what value is, what is valuable, what is valueless, and what is beyond value.

Said value system starts with self-creating a God for the responsibility of maintaining the world of the Ego. This God cannot be responsible for its own mistakes nor can it be responsible for its own ignorance. The prevalent Super Ego must blame something outside of itself for its multiple shortcomings, though. This process, once erected, extends to even the smallest of living things.

Without anything, we would not have a place to return. The Supreme Nothing knows not of the Ego, but the Ego knows of the

Supreme Nothing. The Ego's greatest adversary is the Supreme Nothing.

As long as you feel like nothing, it is not the natural Nothing, for the world of Nothing is complete bliss. Nothing to be concerned with and nothing over which to fret. Everything in its place for its purpose. The Ego cannot claim, own, or control Nothing. Now let us think…should Nothing just be nothing? Said the Ego, concerning Creation, "Let us make man."

The Ego honestly believes it has a relationship with God, but it does not. When it said, "let us make man," it was speaking to itself. It prays to itself, it talks to itself and it rewards itself.

The Egotistical system is like an electrical wire, the natural lifeline of electricity. Electricity is harnessed by the conduit, depending on where the conduit directs the flow, for multiple purposes. Good or bad, electricity can destroy the conduit but the conduit cannot destroy the electricity.

The I Am

"I am" means whatever you perceive me to be, I am. I can be no more than what your Ego allows me to be to you. When the natural spirit of Creation directs you, there is no need to know me---we are one, united in all the ways that the Ego has tried to dissolve.

We call this creative energy love. Ironically, this is the energy on which we humans claim our most profoundly satisfying relationships are based. It is impossible to enter into a state of oneness with separated bodies that have been valued and devalued.

How much of me do I give for a pretty face, eyes, hair, butt, big legs, or good sex? Or how little? These questions can only arise when I am not giving true unconditional love.   "To value the human body is to devalue it." GeLeon

Woman is the mother of human procreation. Experience is attached to innocence. Innocence is attached to experience. Man knows about life because life is tangible. We can see, feel and touch. God we know nothing about, however.

We know about life but we know not what energy created life. Life is all that man can know or identify with. Until he finds or discovers a thing, in his Egotistical mind, man is simply a mass of nothing.

The human cannot imagine a state of nothingness. The Ego will not let him. To the Ego, everything must have labels and titles. Everything must be something, consumed with emotions and with blame.

Lower-class animals have a better understanding of nothing than do human beings. "Nothing" bespeaks less emotion, less wants and less needs. Most animals do not cry when they are hurt or when they are about to die.

If you dedicate yourself to anything you want, in time, you will achieve it because it is all in you. You have created all you know to create. Your heaven and your hell, your beginning and your end, your likes and your dislikes, your reasons, your emotions, and your world.

You can create anything you want in your world, a world of Ego. If you do not or cannot get help inside of you, get it outside of you. You live in a world that supports Ego only. This is the reason there is nothing in the world to which we can ultimately return. For it is from nothing that we came.

Evolutions through osmosis are all very intriguing theories, complete with the idea of single-celled division wherein nothing becomes something and then becomes something more. Creation is interesting, colorful and confusing, when viewed through the murky lens or the musky tomes of the Ego.

I remember reading a book when I was a young man in the South. The book was filled with phrases and terminology. I found the word "vagina" in the book and was excited, as would have been most young men of my age at that time, youth seeking an understanding of the magical activity called sex.

As I read, I was amazed how many different names the vagina had been given over time, only because it was taboo to expose the word vagina to the reading public. The subject, thus the body part, had to be approached underhandedly or through use of code. Why, I wondered, but I was never given a valid reason, so I was left to assume that the reasons were all dirty.

Which makes sense in light of the fact that I had been taught, in early childhood, that all things sexual were dirty. Most of the children, during the 1940s and 1950s in America, would write the word "pussy" on the school's bathroom wall or any other place they thought they could get away with defacing. And pussy was a very dirty word to them. Yet, I did not have a problem with the word pussy because my mother had already taught me, before I journeyed into the school's bathroom, that pussy was the correct term for a cat. I was the odd ball in school.

As I continued to read, I found an interesting metaphor for the vagina. The word was valley. It was explained that many ancient writers had used the word valley as a euphemism for the words vagina and sex. This use of the word valley attracted me because, having been raised in a Christian family, I had learned the Bible's 23rd Psalms.

This biblical chapter deals with the valley of the shadow of death. It was this reference that I could best relate to while reading the definition of vagina. A valley has dirt so, I assumed, this is why my neighbors and their children had considered the vagina dirty. This basic childish acceptance of a typical misunderstanding had been passed down through the generations by the Super Egos controlling the dissemination of information.

Well, since that time, I have been exposed to hundreds of vaginas. Some were clean, some dirty and some complete with their own unique character. But never have I found a vagina to worship or to kill another person over. This is where I become extremely confused.

Man's appreciation for the complete woman has always been much less than what she deserved. Yet, men have killed entire nations over a female's sexuality. Earthly stones have been excavated and polished to adorn her, still without respect for the complete woman.

Recognizing the disparities that man has caused, all for the false esteem he has for woman, prompted me to go back to the vagina. Man, for the most part, could care less who his woman talks to, cooks for, etc., just as long as the other does not touch any part of her body, especially no part of her body near the vagina, i.e. stomach, buttocks, thighs, hips, etc. However, it is not until she shares her vagina with another that man is ready to go to war, and has done so repeatedly throughout history. Which is not to say that she should not share herself; the female, like the male or any other animal, should do what she feels. She should not be defined and valued by her vagina or sexuality.

Of course, most men would deny this judgment (or lack thereof). Mention the mere possibility of vaginal contact being taken away from the male-female relationship and the vast majority of the men will leave their spouses before the month concludes. Lying to self is one of the greatest components of the Ego's campaign.

Subsequently, the vagina is abused: misused, touched, lied on, lied for, worshipped, and condemned to hell. It has been infected with all kinds of diseases and yet it still carries the power that controls the world. Still, without respect to the complete female. Why? Something as pleasurable and destructive as the vagina is something we should learn to understand. Why does it carry so much power?

It is just an Egotistical thing. The Ego knows everything about the human procreative process. It knows that those two lips are the heavenly archway, specifically for the fertilization of human life, so the Ego uses this area of the woman's body as its platform. The vagina is the place of attack on the human procreative process.

The valley of death bespeaks the death of the natural spirit of Creation. Hence, "born in sin and conceived in iniquity." The instant the human body becomes sexual it no longer belongs to the true spiritual self. It then belongs to the human Ego, to be directed, defined and to respond to the kinds of social conditions placed on it.

One of the most beautiful bodies in our existence is, bar none, the human body. Speaking in terms of aesthetics and of engineering, it is simply magnificent. Why then are we taught to be ashamed of it? There is no answer that can correctly and concisely answer this question, other than control.

The dismembering, separation and valuing of body parts by organized societies, into taboo objects, creates masses of flesh to be used and manipulated by Ego. Then, post-use, the individual is taught to be ashamed of his or her body. The person is shrouded in guilt when they allow their bodies to be abused, again, and repeatedly, which makes them even easier to control by the society in which he or she dwells, within the auspices of its norms and mores.

God is beyond the mere idea of nothing because, to the Ego, nothing is something. To the Ego, nothing has perception and perception causes confusion and separation. It is best not to be identified by the Ego.

The spiritual entity we now relate to as a human was once unaware of itself. There was no need for such awareness, as a dog is unaware of its canine status. The human was directed only by the spirit of the Creator. Along with true spiritual love comes choice and, with choice, there was curiosity and desire. Separation followed. The spiritual energy that separated and left the original order is Ego: energy going opposite from the true loving Creator.

To devalue the body, to separate it and to make one part more valuable than another part is both evil and diabolical, but it works for the sake of the Ego's control.

The Creator supports the spirit while the Ego supports the flesh. The spirit knows not of the flesh, no more than does electricity within the wire that houses it does. The Ego's role in this connection is to place its diabolical energies into the conduit, i.e., the human body, via emotional excess. Look around you. Aren't most of the citizens within each civilized society, the ones that you encounter daily, very angry, appearing to lack any appreciation for love?

Social love can never be true spiritual unconditional love because it is a product and a component of the Super Ego. This kind of love has a value system and, along with a value system come conditions, conditions that separate the human from his true spiritual self, conditions that break you down by degrees. You have a different love for different things, even different qualities of love for your own varied body parts.

Love is a solid and complete whole. It cannot be broken down into fractions if the human possesses the spirit of love, and this comes with more understanding and appreciation of self, in Oneness, with Creation and with Nature. You then submit to love, to the one Creator, which is the total embodiment of a unified Creation. This loving spiritual presence only attracts true love. Social love will not work and has never worked. This is the reason we have so many problems and divorces today.

Humans have surrendered to the direction of the Super Ego and have accepted its direction. Some may ask if there is a solution for the problems evident in today's society. Yes, the early churches were once headed in this right direction, but they got off track. The social traditional church was once the center of all communities. As Ego-driven as it was, it was nowhere close to what it is today. It was a place where people assemble to sit, subject to the idea of true love, to hash-out their personal and social problems, even with Egos flaring and prejudices fixed in the minds of many.

The congregants often emerged from these meetings with true solutions for many of their social and personal problems, solutions that affected positive change in their everyday lives. It was because of their willingness to come together in oneness and to discuss problems that gave them an intimate feel for each other. There is nothing worse than thinking and feeling that you are the only one who is maladjusted and who has problems. This type of transparency afforded early congregants a feeling of spiritual oneness, a feeling that extended beyond the church into the communities, effecting and infecting men, women and children.

The spirit of Love must be shown and promoted. When there is an engine, such as what the early churches were, it makes it much easier to want love and to want to be loved. It was not only the churches promoting the spirit of love.

Music and all forms of entertainment were centered on promoting love, togetherness and family commitment. The Ego was not as vigilant back then. Today is seems as if everyone has a big Ego, as if the majority are merely committed to I-ism. Yet, the fundamental ideology of religion has not changed. It is the church leaders and their modes of preaching and of promoting the practicing of the theology that have changed.

The climate in churches today seems to mirror that of the corrupted system that the churches are supposed to be in opposition to, a system that operates from the premise of organized chaos, wherein love is a fantasy and truth is a crime. The church has always been held in high esteem, respected as the house of God, a place where humans went for spiritual support and for true direction. This is not what is being offered by today's churches in my opinion.

Seems to me that the churches have developed the same bad characteristics of today's society: corruption of the individual, self-glorification, separation, and greed, far cries from being the respected entity that even churches of the mid- 20th Century once were. So, if today's churches are the places where people are to go to get spiritual fiber and a true loving spiritual foundation, then we should develop a better understanding of why it is that so many have so little understanding of love and what the results of love should look like.

True spiritual love has no Ego while most church leaders and their congregations are filled with Ego. This fact makes it very difficult to form or to engage in a truly loving, spiritual relationship. Doubt and distrust loom with the first kiss or handshake. Now try imagining the depth of impact this distrust must have in the social marriage.

It is sad that we live in a society where the only idea or place we can get an image of how true love is supposed to look or how true love is supposed to make you feel is at the movies or by reading a romantic novel. Of course, movie and literary images are pretentious and, for the most part, today's loving relationships are as well.

For ages, questions concerning the origins of the homosexual have been raised: whether it is a pretense of the Ego, an abnormality in human development, a physical malady, the result of a psychological breakdown, or possibly a third-gender, one that the collective human Ego has refused to accept. Whether the Ego accepts it or not, homosexuality is a rapidly growing segment of this organized society, a society chock filled with a variety of religions. Some religious sects believe that homosexuality is a curse. Is it a curse to be Black, White, poor, or mentally impaired? True spirituality has not the answer but the Ego will judge, define, accept, or destroy the homosexual, the Black, the White, etc., all based on its own need to satisfy the means to its own end. We do not understand much. Creation is vast and it is mysterious.

Yet, there are things that we do know. A female cannot be a male and a male cannot be a female, no more than a heterosexual can be homosexual. The Ego will lead you to believe you can do and be anything that you chose. We know that is a lie because a man cannot be a dog anymore than he can be a woman. With practice, man can adopt the characteristics of a woman, but he is still a man, just as a heterosexual cannot be a homosexual. This is where the question of the third gender comes into play. There is a natural order to follow, whether we believe it or not.

We should always remember that Ego means energy going opposite, going in the opposite direction from the natural spiritual direction of Creation. Its mission is to separate, to confuse and to cause destruction to anything in its path that fails to submit to its control. This is called the wrath of the Ego.

Homosexuality is an agent of the Ego. Why? Because homosexuality carries all of the characteristics of the Ego. It separates, confuses and promotes destruction. Man having sex with man and woman having sex with woman eventually stops the human procreative process.

It is my spiritual belief that homosexuals do not procreate, that they just have sex, because procreation or intercourse occurs when life (sperm) is placed into another for the sake of reproduction, which does not happen among homosexuals.

Sex is a deceptive pleasure that will and can make one believe that an empty emotion is good. Sex can lead one astray. Sex is an act used to manipulate and to deceive, which often leads humans to believe that they can make love. Love cannot be made. The energy of love existed long before man. Love is an energy to which you must submit yourself.   There is no reason man to man or woman to woman cannot be loving and affectionate, but for a man to believe that another man is a woman or for a woman to believe that another woman is a man bespeaks numerous critical errors along the thought processes. But, the Ego can take you there.

When a male human transmits the most powerful and precious fertilizer in all of human life into a man, the sperm cannot carry out its natural responsibility, the responsibility of furthering human extension.

I have nothing against the way a human esteems himself or herself as long as they are not hurting or harming anyone. Accepting a society where only men are with men and only women are with women? I could never accept this.

All of creation has the right and the choice to choose the style that satisfies them, but no one has the right to stop or to prohibit the extension of life. If same-sex marriage was all we were allowed as a choice of union, it would only be a short time before the human race would become extinct.

Yet, I often wonder…could this be a stage of human evolution? Is the homosexual going through an evolutionary stage, a stage of true oneness? Man and woman in the same body?

Conservative: holding onto traditional attitudes
and values, especially in relation to politics
and religion.

Liberal: ample, full and generous; open-minded;
not strict; favoring political and social reform.

To explore and examine the content of these two words is interesting, especially when these two words lend themselves to the governing and leadership of people.

In the public forum, liberalism is disgusting, embarrassing and disappointing. While watching a televised debate, you would think that the liberal is Satan incarnate, judging by the reaction from the crowd gathered. The cool, calm and collected conservative has and knows exactly what the people under the sound of his voice need.

Try applying a little curiosity to the conservative ideology. Is it possible that a conservative is a person who is perpetually connected to a lineage of Egotistical, conquering, religious and socially manipulative people who devised a system to control the wealth and social direction of the masses forever? If this is the case, it is easy to understand why we have liberals.

Even the most liberal-mannered animal does not see flesh. It sees food when it is hungry. If animals felt about flesh the same way that human beings feel about it, the animal would respond the way humans do. The embodiment of life is contained in many different materials. One is no more important to life than the other, except for the Ego.

The Ego makes all of life less, better or worse. Everything has its own place in time and space, and has the right to survive by whatever means necessary.

The super natural man's choice in favor of his Ego solidified his flesh. Flesh is an accumulative process that took place after man's divorce from the spirit realm. The pre-fall purpose of a body was to function with a true loving purpose. The purpose of each part made the total function equally. Post-separation, though, Ego valued certain parts over others. And his pawn, man, has followed suit.

Naked and nude are products of the Ego, which only means that the body is without true natural creative spirit. The absence of creative spirit promotes many negatives, like desire, gloating, rape, molestation, and shame.

A compliment of the flesh is always expected whether it is a lie or not (vanity). All these things are programmed on the brain by the Ego. Always remember that Ego came from choice. The flesh knows not of the spirit and spirit knows not of the flesh. A baby responds to its body without knowing what a body is. The baby needs love without knowing what love is.

The Creator is the Supreme Energy Force

The rock. Love is the rock, the cultivation, the promotion, the manifestation of God. This happens only when two loving rocks are rubbed together. The resulting friction is called love. The fire that comes from this action is comparable to the energy of the Creator. However, the Creator is a million times more intense.

Love is the same around the world. Love is a language (vibration) everyone understands. Just think for a moment what the world would be if man spent as much time focusing on love and on universal unity as he currently spends focusing on tribal supremacy, money and guns.

Man indicted the true Creator in order to revel in his own holy books. The God of man's own egotistical creation was created for the sake of misleading and of blinding the masses from man's greed and selfishness. The men who steer society achieve this goal by suggesting that the true Creator has chosen ones.

Nothing

In a world built on ever-changing values, there will always be someone who will be deprived or without something to value. Value changes with the whim of the Super Ego, which is the controlling, dominate power at any given time, in time. The Super Ego determines or decides what value is, what is valuable, what is valueless, and what is beyond value.

Said value system starts with self-creating a God for the responsibility of maintaining the world of the Ego. This God cannot be responsible for its own mistakes nor can it be responsible for its own ignorance. The prevalent Super Ego must blame something outside of itself for its multiple shortcomings, though. This process, once erected, extends to even the smallest of living things.

Without anything, we would not have a place to return. The supreme nothing knows not of the Ego but the Ego knows of the supreme nothing. The Ego's greatest adversary is the supreme nothing.

As long as you can feel nothing, it is not the natural Nothing, for the world of Nothing is complete bliss. Nothing to be concerned with and nothing over which to fret. Everything in its place for its purpose.

The Ego cannot claim, own, or control nothing, and these are all characteristics of the Ego.

Now let us think…should nothing just be nothing? Said the Ego, concerning Creation, "Let us make man."

On Having a Personal Relationships with God

No man has a personal relationship with God, no more than he does with any other animal or thing on this planet.

In the true spiritual energy of that force we relate to as God, there is no reason for individuals to have personal relationships with God. God is a unified force. All is one. It is only the ego that separates, labels, defines, and seeks to control.

Ultimately then, the belief and even the desire to have a personal relationship with God is founded on the principle that you have and that another does not, which is distinctly antagonistic to the all is one notion.

On the Indigenous People of the Americas

When God said let us make man, as per the Bible, was that creative energy speaking directly to the elements?

There is one known group of people who spoke to the elements as if to their earthly brethren, exclusively. These people we call American Indians. Could their true connection to the creative process be the reason why all the European powers polarized themselves in order to destroy this group of people? Could it be because they were the most spiritual?

In Europe, the people are divided: European, African, Asian, etc. However, at the time of their most recent discovery on the North American landmass, the indigenous folk, though segregated into tribes, were one group of people who identified with the elements.

Where do We go from Here

For some time now I have pondered how I would end what I knew would be an intensely controversial book. I reached the conclusion that I would finish it just as I started it: matter-of-factly and explicitly. My personal feeling and understanding is that the human being must retract and go back to living by the principle values of natural law, which is the law that nature dictates. We start this process by submitting to the spiritual will of the Creator and nature. There is no other way.

Of course, you will continue to deny, to circumvent and to find other ways and beliefs to make your life easier and more convenient, to satisfy your own selfish ego. What is interesting is that every generation, from the beginning of humanity, submitting to the will of the ego has tried. Humans have tried endlessly to bring love, harmony, peace and tranquility to this selfish, diabolical, chaotic, confused system, but to no avail. The ego does not allow the human to think a loving Oneness. It only allows the human to feel guilt about the selfishness, greed and abuse. This stimulates the selfish human to promote and start a campaign to soothe and patch the negative diabolical condition, to ease and comfort the selfish mind.

In a world where only a few have all and the great majority have so little, the proverbial huddled masses can never achieve the loving peaceful world they claim they're praying, hoping and working toward.

The international system we live today only promotes selfishness and chaos. Moreover and ironically, we have known for a long time that you cannot solve a problem by creating another problem. Yet, we continue to try. You would think that by now man would have figured out that natural law is the only way to go. But no, he has set his own laws and rules for humans and all of life to live by. This makes him his own God.

He ignores his own biological clock and defies all the laws of nature. Then acts shocked and surprised when something disastrous and catastrophic happens, as if he does not know why. This is just an egotistical game to keep the ignorant masses off balance and in fear. Hence, the socio-political, religious, and economic games follow, always dictated and directed by the greedy egotistical minority. It is a system of organized chaos, a system that serves those who are in charge. Those that have the spiritual substance to see a little get chopped-down before they can get started usually imprisoned or killed.

What is funny to me is that for most of my adult life, I have watched and have heard people who live by and who identify with the color Black or White, not even knowing why or where this color identity came from or what it means. Well, I will try to help those people now. White simply means with knowledge, Black without knowledge. The Black must always go to the White for light, for knowledge and for direction for the sake of social survival. Knowledge of self and natural universal law is the only way to balance these playing fields. The single manner in which to achieve said balance is to divorce oneself of ego, then submit to the divine spiritual vibration of the universe. Only then will Black or White, day or night not matter.

We often forget that there is a world of insects, of animals and of people that work and survive while we are sleeping in the dark of night. Their knowledge allows them to make your darkness their light. This transition will enable the human to live and to survive no matter what the conditions are. Your own loving and divine spirit will lead, direct and guide you. Yes, I know this journey back to self will not be easy, primarily because you have forgotten your spiritual will and have placed before it your intellectual ego. Therefore, your spirit has forgotten you.

The intellectual, egotistical mind only deals with logic, reason and profit. If I am not gaining or getting something profitable out of it, then forget or fuck it. The expressions "Fuck" and "Fuck it" are direct responses whenever one is being forced or reminded that the purity of the human is being interfered or tampered with. The purity or the Christ factor in all of humanity is where the presence of God or the loving spirit of oneness lives and exists.

Fornication under carnal knowledge was and is a campaign to etch the truth and awareness of God's will and presence away from the mind of the human being. The campaign then places before humanity, in the place of the Creator, an artificial and intellectual god, one created within the selfish egotistical minds of men. Whenever a person's mind is absent of the loving spirit of Oneness, we all experience the chaos that we see today. Man cannot continue to rely on the ego for his direction and survival and still achieve the loving environment that he claims he is trying to achieve.

You see, the expression "Fuck" is considered derogatory only because it exposes what the fabricated egotistical system has and is doing to you (the human being). Those who do not or who have not yet used this expression are consumed and are blinded by the mission to etch God completely out.

May the Creator be with you.

GLOSSARY OF TERMS

ANGEL / DEVIL – manifestation or apparition of the ego; an egotistical product of despair, fear and deprivation.

CHOICE – A child comes from a world of darkness into a world of light, revealing an array of colors, which stimulates feelings. Whichever is the most dominate color in its immediate environment will create a dominant feeling in the child and, from that time on, he will relate his most powerful feeling with that color.

EGO – etching God out; going away from the loving Oneness of Creation; taking the true God of love and Oneness off the mind and out of the picture of life.

ENERGY – opposing spiritual friction; created by opposing love. It runs out. Everything natural has spirit while everything unnatural has energy.

EXCITEMENT – an event that is an explosion in time; a multi-colored explosion. Excitement is your choice of color.

FUCK – to penetrate anyone's personal spiritual sanctity for a loveless purpose.

GOD – the total loving and spiritual unification and embodiment of creation; that which can be imagined and not; an immense spiritual force so powerful humans can only conceive fractions of it; man can never be almighty God. He is only one component of Creation. God can be everywhere and anything, only because it is.

HATE – lack of love; confusion; perpetually disgruntled; disliking one's true spiritual self; egotistical impairment.

LOVE – a vibration free of selfishness; absolute protection from evil; a spirit that supports caring, equality and Oneness for all of humanity and Creation.

MATING – a spiritual ritual; a coming together of man and woman to enter into each other to exemplify the joy of Oneness for the purpose of extending life.

SEX – a selective choice to seduce and to manipulate for a selfish purpose; selfish physical gratification.

SUPER EGO – absolute selfish control; caring about only self- improvement, ethnocentric in opinion; egomaniacal.

THE SPIRIT – the loving creative force that never runs out or ends; a force field committed only to the most powerful vibration in the universe, Love. This vibration is more relentless, resilient and everlasting that any energy force.

VIBRATION – a silent force capable of being felt by the spiritually sound; the vehicle by which love travels.